CHILDREN'S ISSUES, LAWS AND PROGRAMS

CHILD EXPLOITATION PREVENTION AND INTERDICTION

CHILDREN'S ISSUES, LAWS AND PROGRAMS

Additional books in this series can be found on Nova's website under the Series tab.

Additional E-books in this series can be found on Nova's website under the E-books tab.

LAW, CRIME AND LAW ENFORCEMENT

Additional books in this series can be found on Nova's website under the Series tab.

Additional E-books in this series can be found on Nova's website under the E-books tab.

CHILDREN'S ISSUES, LAWS AND PROGRAMS

CHILD EXPLOITATION PREVENTION AND INTERDICTION

ANDREW K. CLAMPET
EDITOR

Nova Science Publishers, Inc.
New York

For permission to use material from this book please contact us:
Telephone 631-231-7269; Fax 631-231-8175
Web Site: http://www.novapublishers.com

NOTICE TO THE READER

LIBRARY OF CONGRESS CATALOGING-IN-PUBLICATION DATA
Child exploitation prevention and interdiction / editors, Andrew K. Clampet.
p. cm. -- (Children's issues, laws and programs)
Includes bibliographical references and index.
ISBN 978-1-61122-854-0 (softcover : alk. paper)
1. Teenage sex offenders--United States. I. Clampet, Andrew K.
HV9067.S48.C47 2011
362.76'5610973--dc22
2010046849

Published by Nova Science Publishers, Inc. † New York

CONTENTS

PREFACE

This book presents a synthesis of major studies on child exploitation and an annotated bibliography. Topics discussed in this compilation include: Internet crimes against children; the role of the family and caregivers in preventing children from becoming victims of sexual abuse; the incidence of sexual solicitation according to demographics and social characteristics and the role that law enforcement can play in prosecuting predators and evaluating the effectiveness of their investigations.

Chapter 1- In 2009, the Federal Research Division of the Library of Congress prepared a synthesis of major studies surrounding Internet crimes against children using funding from the National Institute of Justice. As previously noted, the inclusion of any study or project does not indicate that the Department supports the conclusions of such study or project.

Chapter 2- As noted in the body of the Report, the Act requested that the Department provide a review of relevant research in the child exploitation field. A listing of Department-funded research is below. It is important to note that the inclusion of any study or research project in this Report is not intended to convey support for the findings of any of such study or research project. A synthesis of major studies, and an accompanying annotated bibliography, can be found in Appendix F.

The Office of Juvenile Justice and Delinquency Prevention is currently funding the following studies / research projects related to child exploitation. The projects are on varying timelines and will have results / research reports available at varying times.

A National Study of Internet-Facilitated Commercial Sexual Exploitation of Children (IF-CSEC) in the Criminal Justice System is a project designed by the awardee, the University of New Hampshire. The award has a start date of

1/1/2007 and end date of 12/31/2009. This study of Internet-facilitated CSEC (IF-CSEC) crimes focuses on the future directions of commercial sexual exploitation of children and youth by looking at how offenders use the Internet to facilitate CSEC in a broad range of cases handled by law enforcement agencies, including child prostitution, trafficking, sex tourism, child pornography and other CSEC crimes. It brings together an experienced research partner with a strong research background in child sexual exploitation, the Crimes against Children Research Center, and a law enforcement partner with a high degree of expertise in the use of Internet technology in sexual exploitation crimes, the Internet Crimes Against Children Task Forces

In: Child Exploitation Prevention and Interdiction ISBN: 978-1-61122-854-0
Editor: Andrew K. Clampet

Chapter 1

SYNTHESIS OF MAJOR STUDIES*

Library of Congress/National Institute of Justice

In 2009, the Federal Research Division of the Library of Congress prepared a synthesis of major studies surrounding Internet crimes against children using funding from the National Institute of Justice. As previously noted, the inclusion of any study or project does not indicate that the Department supports the conclusions of such study or project.

Research conducted relative to Internet crimes against children can be grouped into several subtopics: unwanted solicitation for sexual contact or pictures; pornography (children as the subject); harassment and bullying; and unwanted exposure to sexually explicit material. Many of the studies described in this document have been conducted by researchers affiliated with the Crimes Against Children Research Center at the University of New Hampshire who extrapolated data from the First (2000) and Second (2005) Youth Internet Safety Survey. These surveys canvassed a nationally representative sample of 1,500 youth ages 10 to 17 to determine the incidence and risk factors of youth exposure to sexual material on the Internet. Researchers also extrapolated data from the National Juvenile Online Victimization Study, which was intended to estimate the incidence of Internet sex crimes against minors occurring during a one-year period (2000–200 1) that were known to law enforcement officials. This bibliography reviews the findings of the studies conducted using these

* This is an edited, reformatted and augmented edition of a joint report compiled by the Library of Congress and National Institute of Justice.

surveys, as well as other surveys conducted for the purpose of identifying the patterns and frequency of criminal use of the Internet involving children. The bibliography also reviews the results of focus-group studies, literature reviews, and reports commissioned by the U.S. Congress.

The purpose of the studies, surveys, and reports reviewed herein was multifaceted. Researchers primarily sought to determine how frequently children view sexually explicit material online and are approached for sexual activity online, as well as the demographics of the vulnerable populations. They also wanted to identify what specific crimes were being committed, and by whom, the role law enforcement plays in curtailing and preventing these activities, and what influence pornography and sexualized material have on the moral values and sexual attitudes of children and youth. They looked at broader issues as well: how children use the Internet generally (as compared with adults) and what role family dynamics and the parent–child relationship play in the prevention of Internet crime. Some of the studies examine a particular aspect of Internet crimes against children. For example, Patricia M. Greenfield, in testimony before Congress, addressed the role of peer-to-peer file-sharing networks. She concludes that the networks are part of a pervasive, sexualized media environment that leads to inadvertent exposure of children and youth to pornography and other adult sexual content. In 2003 the U.S. General Accounting Office reported that child pornography is easily found and downloaded from peer-to-peer networks, confirming observations of the National Center for Missing & Exploited Children.

Other researchers looked at one aspect of online sexual exploitation —the grooming of children by adult predators. Ilene R. Berson and Duncan Brown, in their articles, describe how online predators use deceptive techniques to gain a young child's trust and manipulate him or her into viewing pornography and agreeing to a personal meeting. Janis Wolak, David Finkelhor, and Kimberly J. Mitchell, in "Internet-Initiated Sex Crimes Against Minors," describe characteristics of interactions between Internet predators and their juvenile victims. A year-long survey conducted in 2001 of 129 Internet-initiated sex crimes involving victims age 17 or younger found that face-to-face meetings had occurred in 74 percent of the cases, and 93 percent of those encounters had included sexual contact. Seventy-five percent of the victims were girls. The same authors, writing in "Trends in Youth Reports of Sexual Solicitations, Harassment and Unwanted Exposure to Pornography on the Internet," report survey results indicating that predators use less deception to befriend their online victims than experts had thought. A large majority of the victims who responded to the survey had willingly met and had sexual encounters with the predators.

Communication technologies, such as computers and cell phones, and social-networking sites like My Space enable the rapid creation and dissemination of harassing and pornographic text, pictures, and video. Paris S. and Robert D. Strom note that whereas adults generally use technology only as a tool, adolescents consider technology, including text messaging and chat rooms, to be an essential part of their social life. The results of a 2007 online survey of more than 40,000 students ranging from kindergarten through twelfth grade (Samuel C. McQuade and Neel Sampat) indicate that children begin using the Internet at kindergarten age or younger and that online activities of children in the grades covered by this study include inappropriate behavior and exposure to inappropriate content. Wolak, Mitchell, and Finkelhor note that Internet use by youth age 12 to 17 increased from 73 percent in 2000 to 87 percent in 2005. Cyberbullying (bullying by means of electronic communication, such as instant messaging, e-mail, chat rooms, and cell phones) and victimization begin as early as second grade for some children, and by middle school, students as a group experience or engage in all known forms of cyber abuse and online aggression. Online exchange of sexually explicit content typically begins in middle school.

Researchers (Wilson Huang, Matthew Earl Leopard, and Andrea Brockman) have concluded that the rapid growth of online sexual exploitation of children can be linked to increased Internet accessibility and anonymity, commercialization of exploitative media, and digitization in the production and dissemination of images. These researchers found that, despite legislative initiatives intended to keep pace with the incidence of this type of crime against children, the nature and distribution of child pornography, as well as the characteristics of offenders and victims alike, have remained similar over time and across a wide sample of studies. A 2007 staff report of the U.S. House Energy and Commerce Committee placed the issue of Internet crimes against children in perspective. The committee found that the number of sexually explicit images of children on the Internet was increasing, and that victims were typically younger and the images more violent than in previous years. At the time the report was written, it was estimated that Web sites hosted in the United States accounted for more than half of the child pornography on the Internet, and that commercially available child pornography on the Internet comprised a multibillion-dollar per year industry.

INCIDENCE OF INTERNET ACTIVITY

Researchers studied the frequency of exposure to sexually explicit material by boys and girls, how often the youths posted this material, and the frequency of online bullying and harassment activity. Kenzie A. Cameron and Laura F. Salazar found in their study of adolescents ages 14 to 17 that among the participants who reported incidences of exposure to sexually explicit Web sites, most occurred accidentally or unintentionally, via unsolicited e-mails (10 to 20 per day) containing explicit content or links to explicit material. Chiara Sabina, Wolak, and Finkelhor, using data compiled from an online survey of more than 500 college students, found that 72.8 percent (93.2 percent of the male students and 62.1 percent of the female students) of the sample group reported that they had viewed online pornography before the age of 18. Males were found to be more likely to view pornography frequently and to view a variety of images, while females were more likely to be involuntarily exposed to pornography. Wolak, Mitchell, and Finkelhor, in "Unwanted and Wanted Exposure to Online Pornography in a National Sample of Youth Internet Users" reported findings of data taken from the Second (2005) Youth Internet Safety Survey regarding exposure to online pornography. They found that 42 percent of a sample of 10- to 17year-old Internet users had viewed online pornography during the previous year. Of that 42 percent, 66 percent reported that they had not sought or desired the exposure to pornography.

A survey of more than 1,000 teens and young adults conducted in 2008 and reported by the National Campaign to Prevent Teen and Unplanned Pregnancy revealed that 20 percent of the teens had sent or posted nude or seminude pictures or video of themselves, and 11 percent of young adolescent girls (ages 13 to 16) had done so. Thirty-nine percent of teens reported sending sexually suggestive text messages ("sexting"), and 48 percent of teens reported having received such messages. Mitchell, Finkelhor, and Wolak, in "Online Requests for Sexual Pictures from Youth," used data from the 2005 youth survey to assess the incidence of soliciting youth to produce sexually explicit images and post or transmit them online. The authors found that 13 percent of the youth in the study population had received unwanted sexual solicitations over the Internet, and although 4 percent of the youth had received an online request to send a sexual picture of themselves, only one complied. Thirteen percent of the overall survey group received unwanted sexual solicitations that included requests for pictures.

Social-networking Web sites, such as Facebook, My Space, and You Tube, are often used by young persons to harass their peers. Michele L. Ybarra and Mitchell, in "Prevalence and Frequency of Internet Harassment Instigation," extrapolated data from the 2005 youth survey to identify the frequency with which youth ages 10 to 17 engaged in online harassment activity. They found that almost 30 percent of youth had harassed others online during the previous year: 6 percent had frequently harassed others via the Internet; 6 percent had occasionally harassed others online; and 17 percent had harassed others a limited number of times. Amanda Lenhart reports the results of a Parents and Teens 2006 Survey tabulating the incidence of cyberbullying. Researchers found that 32 percent of more than 900 youth (ages 12 to 17) Internet users surveyed had been harassed online. Of this group, 38 percent of the girls and 41 percent of the girls ages 15 to 17 had experienced online harassment, as compared with 26 percent of the boys. Thirty- nine percent of teenagers who provided personal information on a social networking site were the target of harassment. Robin M. Kowalski and Susan P. Limber studied the prevalence of electronic bullying (defined as bullying that takes place through Internet chat rooms, e-mail, instant messaging, or Web sites) among middle school students. Their research found that 11 percent of the students reported being electronically bullied one or more times in the previous two months; 7 percent stated that they had bullied others electronically and had been the victims of electronic bullying; and 4 percent reported that they had bullied others electronically but had not been victims. Chris Moessner reported the results of a national survey of more than 800 children ages 13 to 17 measuring adolescent reaction to cyberbullying, which is defined as the use of the Internet, cell phones, or other technology to send or post text or images intended to hurt or embarrass another person. More than 43 percent of the teenagers in the survey reported that they had experienced cyberbullying in the previous year, with the most common occurrence among those 15 and 16 years old.

Role of the Family and Other Caregivers

Researchers looked at the role parents and other caregivers can play in preventing children from becoming victims of Internet crime, emphasizing that better education programs are needed and that strong communication between adults and children is critical. The study by Chang-Hoan Cho and Hongsik John Cheon found that parents generally underestimate their children's exposure to negative material on the Internet, when in fact children encounter negative content frequently. McQuade and Sampat found that 66 percent of high school students reported that their parents provided no supervision of Internet activities. Cho and Cheon confirm the findings of earlier studies that parents of families exhibiting high levels of cohesion perceive greater control and understanding of their children's Internet use. Similarly, Greenfield found that a warm, communicative parent–child relationship, appropriate sex education, and parental participation in children's Internet activities are critical factors in protecting children from adverse effects of exposure to explicit sexual material. Moe ssner, in his study of a national survey of cyberbullying by those 13 to 17 years old, suggests that parents can help their children avoid cyberbullies by setting expectations for online behavior and monitoring children's Internet activities. Stefan C. Dombrowski, Karen L. Gischlar, and Theo Durst note that caregivers can access various software tools such as firewall security barriers to monitor a child's online activity and help protect him or her from accessing unsafe Web sites.

In addition, they recommend that parents discuss Internet dangers, monitor Internet usage, supervise Internet friendships, and establish an Internet-use contract with their child. Whitney Roban, reporting a 2001 study of more than 1,000 girls ages 13 to 18, concluded that not all girls are receiving pertinent Internet-safety information from their parents, and that half the girls in the study reported breaking Internet rules set by their parents. The study concludes that parents should try to be more proactive in their relationship with their daughters; if they develop a greater understanding of their daughters' online lives, they can better help them navigate negative Internet experiences. The Internet Safety Technical Task Force, in its final report, concludes that in order to address the problem of online safety for minors, adults must use the numerous technologies intended to enhance Internet safety, together with parental oversight, education, social services, and law enforcement.

Demographics and Social Characteristics

Some researchers categorized the incidence of sexual solicitation, unwanted exposure to pornography, and bullying/harassment according to demographic and gender indicators. According to Mitchell, Finkelhor and Wolak, in their evaluation of the second youth survey ("Online Requests for Sexual Pictures from Youth"), youth who are female, black, have close online relationships, or engage in online sexual behavior are more likely than others to receive solicitations for sexual pictures. In another study ("Trends in Youth Reports"), these same authors, extrapolating survey data, found that black youth and low-income families had experienced an increased incidence of sexual solicitation. Unwanted exposure to pornography had increased among those 10 to 12 years old and 16 to 17 years old, boys, and white, non- Hispanic youth. These authors found in another study ("Victimization of Youths on the Internet") that predators had targeted girls for sexual solicitation at almost twice the rate of boys, and youth who were at least 15 years old accounted for nearly two-thirds of incidents of unwanted exposure. They also found that young people at risk for unwanted sexual solicitation, harassment, and exposure to sexual content on the Internet tend to be troubled, older adolescents who use the Internet frequently and engage in high-risk online behavior, although those youth not falling into these categories are at risk as well.

Ybarra and Mitchell studied the social characteristics of offline and online aggressors. Analyzing the results of the first youth survey (2000), they found that although boys commit most incidents of offline harassment, the number of boys and girls who use the Internet to harass their peers is almost equal. Both offline bullies and youth who harass others online often have multiple psychosocial issues: 51 percent of all bullies had been victims of traditional bullying, 44 percent had a poor relationship with their caregiver, 37 percent showed a pattern of delinquency, and 32 percent were frequent substance abusers.

These same authors, in "Exposure to Internet Pornography among Children and Adolescents," found that the majority of youth who reported seeking pornography online and offline were male; only 5 percent of females reported having looked for pornography. The majority (87 percent) of those who reported having sought sexual images were older than 14.

Law Enforcement

Researchers studied the role that law enforcement can play in prosecuting online predators and evaluated the effectiveness of their investigations. Brown, in his guide for prosecutors seeking to prosecute online predators, recommends that law enforcement officers acquire probative evidence against the perpetrator, collecting and preserving all evidence of grooming (preparing children for sexual exploitation), such as pornography, Web cameras, and other electronic equipment, in order that prosecutors can present the evidence at trial to show the perpetrator's motivation. Mitchell, Wolak, and Finkelhor, in "Police Posing as Juveniles Online to Catch Sex Offenders," used data from the National Juvenile Online Victimization (NJOV) Study to evaluate the effectiveness of proactive online investigations, in which police investigators use the Internet—posing as minors and often assuming a different gender—to communicate via chat rooms, e-mail, and instant messaging, to interdict youth enticement and child pornography. These investigations were used in 25 percent of all arrests for Internet crimes against children, and resulted in offenders entering pleas in 91 percent of cases. Melissa Wells, along with Finkelhor, Wolak, and Mitchell, used the results of the NJOV Study to highlight two problems faced by law enforcement agencies in making arrests for child pornography: the nature of the child pornography portrayed in the confiscated images may not fit the definitions of existing statutes, and investigators may not be able to determine the age of the children in the images with certainty.

Other problems in law enforcement are discussed in the U.S. House Energy and Commerce Committee staff report. Researchers found that although law enforcement agencies at the state level prosecute 70 percent of all cases involving sexual exploitation of children over the Internet, there is a wide discrepancy among state criminal codes in their treatment of these offenses and in their sentencing practices. Encryption methods, such as anonymizers, significantly interfere with law enforcement's ability to investigate and bring charges against offenders.

Impact of Internet Crimes

Most of the research on Internet crimes against children has focused on quantifying the prevalence of illegal activities and identifying ways of preventing future activities. However, a few researchers have attempted to assess the psychological impact these activities have on young persons, as well the implications for other criminal activity. For example, Cameron and Salazar, in their study of adolescents ages 14 to 17 who regularly use the Internet, determined that both boys and girls reported their perception that exposure to sexually explicit material had no effect on their personal views of either gender or of relationships. Similarly, Sabina, Wolak, and Finkelhor found in their study of college students that only a minority reported that viewing online pornography before the age of 18 had strongly affected their attitudes or emotions about sexuality. On the other hand, Greenfield, who studied the unintended exposure of young people to pornography through peer-to-peer file-sharing networks, concludes that evidence supports the thesis that pornography and sexualized material can influence the moral values, sexual activity, and sexual attitudes of children and youth, including their attitudes toward sexual violence.

Neil Malamuth and Mark Huppin studied the relationship between pornography and child molestation. They found that although child molesters (individuals who commit sexual acts against children) use pornography to groom potential victims, pedophiles (individuals who are sexually aroused by children) are less likely to molest a child after viewing pornography. The researchers conclude that whether exposure to a real or virtual child affects a person's behavior depends on a number of risk factors, and that, therefore, no strong cause and effect exists between viewing child pornography and committing sexual molestation of a child.

Michael Bourke and Andres Hernandez, in a very recent study on the relationship between the viewing and collection of child pornography and the commission of a sexual contact crime against a child, reach a different conclusion. The results of their research indicated that following participation in a treatment program, child pornography offenders admitted to a significantly greater number of sexual abuse crimes than before they were sentenced. Persons in this study group who had used the Internet to access child pornography were also significantly more likely to have committed a sexual contact crime. The authors conclude that persons using the Internet to commit child pornography offenses may also be undetected child molesters.

Need for Further Research and Changes in Approach to the Problem

Based on research conducted using various surveys, focus-group studies, and other data compilations, the authors of the studies reviewed in this bibliography made several recommendations regarding the need for additional research in the area of Internet crimes against children. In addition, they suggest ways in which parents, educators, and law enforcement officials can gain greater awareness of the magnitude of this problem, and consequently be better able to stem the proliferation of sexually explicit material through the Internet. Many of the recommendations specifically directed to parents are discussed above in the section "Role of the Family and Other Caregivers."

Ybarra and Mitchell, analyzing data from the first (2000) youth survey, identified several areas warranting further research: the small group of females intentionally seeking pornography; the link between purposeful exposure to pornography and emotional challenges, such as major depression or a poor emotional bond with a caregiver; the role of alcohol in delinquent behavior involving intentional seeking of pornography; and whether or not the Internet has become a more common mode of intentional exposure to pornography among adolescents than the viewing of sexually explicit material offline. Mitchell, Finkelhor, and Wolak, in "Online Requests for Sexual Pictures from Youth," recommend that pediatric and adolescent health professionals be aware of the incidence of online requests for sexual pictures of youths and of the Internet's role in expanding the production of child pornography. These same authors, in their study "Trends in Youth Reports of Sexual Solicitations, Harassment and Unwanted Exposure to Pornography on the Internet," recommend that caregivers, social service providers, and law enforcement agents target minority and less affluent populations for prevention programs, to protect them from online harassment and from predators.

In their study of Internet-initiated sex crimes against minors, these authors acknowledge that Internet victim-prevention programs have emphasized the dangers of predator deception but find that educators fail to address the problems of young persons who are befriended by adult predators online and willingly meet with them to have voluntary sexual relationships. In another study using data extrapolated from the first (2000) youth survey, these authors concluded that a major flaw in the 2000 study—the lack of standardized, validated procedures for collecting data on children exposed to sexual material on the Internet—indicated the urgent need to collect further evidence to inform public policy aimed at protecting youth from unwanted exposure to Internet pornography.

SOURCES FOR SYNTHESIS OF MAJOR STUDIES

[1] Berson, Ilene R. (2003). "Grooming Cybervictims: The Psychological Effects of Online Exploitation for Youth." *Journal of School Violence, 2*, no. 1, 9–18. http://www.cs.auckland.ac.nz/ ~john/NetSafe/I.Be

rson.pdf (accessed March 20, 2009).

[2] Bourke, Michael L. & Andres E. Hernandez. (2009). "The 'Butner Study' Redux: A Report of the Incidence of Hands-on Child Victimization by Child Pornography Offenders." *Journal of Family Violence*, *24*, no. 3 (April): 183–93.

[3] Brown, Duncan. (2009). "Developing Strategies for Collecting and Presenting Grooming Evidence in a High Tech World." Update (National Center for Prosecution of Child Abuse), 2001, 1. http:www.ndaa. org/publications/newsletters/update_volume_1 4_number_1 1_200 1 .html (accessed March 24).

[4] Cameron, Kenzie A. & Laura F. Salazar. (2005). "Adolescents' Experience with Sex on the Web: Results from Online Focus Groups." *Journal of Adolescence*, *28*, no. 4, 535–40.

[5] Cho, Chang-Hoan & Hongsik John Cheon. (2009). "Children's Exposure to Negative Internet Content: Effects of Family Context." *Journal of Broadcasting and Electronic Media*, *49*, no. 4 (December 2005).
http://findarticles.com/p/articles/mi_m6836/is_4_49/ai_n25120984/
(accessed May).

[6] Dombrowski, Stefan C., Karen L. Gischlar & Theo Durst. (2007). "Safeguarding Young People from Cyber Pornography and Cyber Sexual Predation: A Major Dilemma of the Internet." *Child Abuse Review*, *16*, no. 3, 153–70.

[7] Greenfield, Patricia M. (2004). "Inadvertent Exposure to Pornography on the Internet: Implications of Peer-to-Peer File-Sharing Networks for Child Development and Families." *Applied Developmental Psychology, 25,* 741–50.

[8] Huang, Wilson, Mathew Earl Leopard & Andrea Brockman. (2009). "Internet Child Sexual Exploitation: Offenses, Offenders, and Victims." In Crimes of the Internet, edited by Frank Schmalleger and Michael Pittaro, 43–65. Upper Saddle River, NJ: Pearson Education.

[9] Internet Safety Technical Task Force. (2008). "Enhancing Child Safety and Online Technologies: Final Report of the Internet Safety Technical Task Force to the Multi-State Working Group on Social Networking of State Attorneys General of the United States." Report, Internet Safety Technical Task Force, Berkman Center for Internet and Society, Harvard University, Cambridge, MA, December 31. http://cyber.law.harvard.edu/ pubrelease/isttf/ (accessed January 5, 2009).

[10] Kowalski, Robin, M. & Susan, P. Limber. (2007). "Electronic Bullying

Among Middle School Students." *Journal of Adolescent Health, 41*, no. 6, S22–S30. *http://www.wctlaw.com/CM/Custom/Electronic% 20Bullying% 20Among%20Middle%20School%* 20Students.pdf (accessed March 24, 2009).

[11] Lenhart, Amanda. (2007). "Cyberbullying and Online Teens." Research Memo, Pew/Internet and American Life Project, Pew Research Center, Washington, DC, June 27. http://www.pewinternet.org/~/media 20Memo.pdf.pdf (accessed March 23, 2009).

[12] Malamuth, Neil & Mark Huppin. (2006–2007). "Drawing the Line on Virtual Child Pornography: Bringing the Law in Line with the Research Evidence." *New York University Review of Law and Social Change, 31*, 773–827.

[13] McQuade, Samuel C., III & Neel Sampat. (2008). "Survey of Internet and At-Risk Behaviors: Undertaken by School Districts of Monroe County, New York, May 2007 to June 2008 and October 2007 to January 2008." Report, Center for Multidisciplinary Studies, Rochester Institute of Technology, Rochester, New York, June 18.

[14] Moessner, Chris. (2009). "Cyberbullying." Trends and Tudes, April 2007, 1–4. *http://www. harrisinteractive.com/news/newsletters/k12 news/HI_ TrendsTudes_2007_v06_i04.pdf* (accessed March 23).

[15] Mitchell, Kimberly J., David Finkelhor & Janis Wolak. (2007). "Online Requests for Sexual Pictures from Youth: Risk Factors and Incident Characteristics." *Journal of Adolescent Health, 41*, no. 2, 196–203. http://www.unh.edu/ccrc/pdf/CV155.pdf (accessed March 27, 2009).

[16] Mitchell, Kimberly, J., David Finkelhor, and Janis Wolak. "Victimization of Youths on the Internet." *Journal of Aggression, Maltreatment and Trauma,* 8, nos. 1–2 (May 2003): 1–3 9.

[17] Mitchell, Kimberly J., Janis Wolak & David Finkelhor. (2005). "Police Posing as Juveniles Online to Catch Sex Offenders: Is It Working?" Sexual Abuse: *A Journal of Research and Treatment, 17*, no. 3 (July): 241–67. http://www.unh.edu/ccrc/pdf/CV82.pdf (accessed March 28, 2009).

[18] Mitchell, Kimberly J., Janis Wolak & David Finkelhor. (2007). "Trends in Youth Reports of Sexual Solicitations, Harassment and Unwanted Exposure to Pornography on the Internet." *Journal of Adolescent Health, 40*, no. 2, 116–26. http://www.unh.edu/ccrc/pdf/ CV135.pdf (accessed March 24, 2009).

[19] Roban, Whitney. (2002). "The Net Effect: Girls and New Media." Executive Summary, Girl Scout Research Institute, Girl Scouts of the

United States of America, New York,. *http://www.girlscouts.org/research/pdf/net_effect.pdf* (accessed March 20, 2009).

[20] Sabina, Chiara, Janis Wolak & David Finkelhor. (2008). "Rapid Communication: The Nature and Dynamics of Internet Pornography Exposure for Youth." *CyberPsychology and Behavior, 11*, no. ,: 691–93.

[21] Strom, Paris S. & Robert D. Strom. "Cyberbullying by Adolescents: A Preliminary Assessment." *Educational Forum*, *70*, no. 1 (Fall), 21–36.

[22] U.S. Congress. House of Representatives. (2005). Committee on Energy and Commerce. Subcommittee on Oversight and Investigations. "Sexual Exploitation of Children over the Internet." 109th Cong., 2d sess., January 2007. Staff Report. *http://republicans.energycommerce*.house.gove/1 08/News/0 1 032007_Report.pdf (accessed May 2009).

[23] U. S. General Accounting Office. (2003). "File-Sharing Programs: Peer-to-Peer Networks Provide Ready Access to Child Pornography." Report to the Chairman and Ranking Minority Member, Committee on Government Reform, House of Representatives, no. GAO–03–351, Washington, DC.

[24] Wells, Melissa, David Finkelhor, Janis Wolak & Kimberly J. Mitchell. (2007). "Defining Child Pornography: Law Enforcement Dilemmas in Investigations of Internet Child Pornography Possession." *Police Practice and Research, 8*, no. 3 (July), 269–82.

[25] Wolak, Janis, David Finkelhor & Kimberly J. Mitchell. (2009). "Internet-Initiated Sex Crimes Against Minors: Implications for Prevention Based on Findings from a National Study." *Journal of Adolescent Health, 35*, no. 5 (2004): 11–20. *http://www.unh.edu/ccrc/pdf/CV71.pdf* (accessed March 23).

[26] Wolak, Janis, Kimberly J. Mitchell & David Finkelhor. (2007). "Unwanted and Wanted Exposure to Online Pornography in a National Sample of Youth Internet Users." *Pediatrics*, *119*, no. 2, 247–57.

[27] Ybarra, Michele L. & Kimberly J. Mitchell. (2005). "Exposure to Internet Pornography among Children and Adolescents: A National Survey." *CyberPsychology and Behavior, 8*, no. 5, 473–86.

[28] Ybarra, Michele L. & Kimberly J. Mitchell. (2007). "Prevalence and Frequency of Internet Harassment Instigation: Implications for Adolescent Health." *Journal of Adolescent Health,41*, no. ,: 189–95. http://www.unh.edu/ccrc/pdf/CV157.pdf (accessed March 20, 2009).

ANNOTATED BIBLIOGRAPHY

Child Pornography/Exposure to Sexually Explicit Material

Bourke, Michael L., and Andres E. Hernandez. "The 'Butner Study' Redux: A Report of the Incidence of Hands-on Child Victimization by Child Pornography Offenders." Journal of Family Violence 24, no. 3 (April 2009): 183–93.

The study sought to determine whether a person who viewed and/or collected child pornography was at low risk of committing a sexual contact crime against a child, or if such a person is a contact sex offender whose crimes have gone undetected. The study consisted of two analyses. In the first analysis, the authors examined information about offenders' criminal sexual histories collected prior to and following participation in a treatment program. Following treatment, offenders admitting to contact crimes increased from 26 percent to 85 percent, and the average number of victims per offender increased from 1.88 to 13.56. The second analysis examined only the subset of offenders acknowledging at the end of treatment that they had committed at least one contact crime against a child. The results showed an increase across all categories compared to what was known at the time of sentencing: the number of offenders acknowledging abuse of both pre- and post-pubescent victims increased 47 percent; those admitting to have victimized both males and females increased from 15 to 40 percent; and among offenders without any known victims at the time of sentencing, 24 percent acknowledged victims of both genders, and 48 percent admitted to contact crimes against pre- and post-pubescent victims. The authors also found that persons in this sample group who had used the Internet to access child pornography were significantly more likely to have committed a contact crime. From this result, they concluded that this population of offenders may also be undetected child molesters.

Huang, Wilson, Mathew Earl Leopard, and Andrea Brockman. "Internet Child Sexual Exploitation: Offenses, Offenders, and Victims." In Crimes of the Internet, edited by Frank Schmalleger and Michael Pittaro, 43–65. Upper Saddle River, NJ: Pearson Education, 2009.

The authors of this chapter in a book about various Internet crimes discuss factors contributing to the rapid growth of online sexual exploitation of children, linking it to increased Internet accessibility and anonymity, commercialization of exploitative media, and digitization in the production and dissemination of images. The authors found that, despite legislative initiatives intended to keep pace with the incidence of this type of crime against children, the nature and distribution of child pornography, as well as the characteristics of offenders and victims alike, have remained similar over time and across a wide sample of studies. The chapter includes an overview of legislative developments and case law in this area, including the various legal definitions of what constitutes child pornography. The authors discuss types of images of child abuse, distinguishing between images, pornography, and erotica produced commercially and those that are homemade. Homemade images, although never produced for commercial profit, circulate repeatedly in the pedophile community, forming a substantial portion of currently circulating images. The authors compare the findings of numerous recent studies, discussing the behavior of perpetrators, the reasons they collect images of child abuse, the personal characteristics of individuals who produce and collect child pornography, and the personal characteristics of their victims. Finally, the authors highlight new federal legislation, as well as new Internet developments, noting problems that have arisen with the use of social-networking sites like My Space and the use of webcams and similar technologies that blend the roles of the producer and the victim of child pornography.

Internet Safety Technical Task Force. "Enhancing Child Safety and Online Technologies: Final Report of the Internet Safety Technical Task Force to the Multi-State Working Group on Social Networking of State Attorneys General of the United States." Report, Internet Safety Technical Task Force, Berkman Center for Internet and Society, Harvard University, Cambridge, MA, December 31, 2008. http://cyber.law.harvard.edu/ pubrelease/isttf/ (accessed January 5, 2009).

In this final report, the Internet Safety Technical Task Force summarizes and analyzes two previous documents produced by the Task Force—a literature review of relevant research about the online safety of youth in the United States and a review of 40 technologies intended to increase online safety. The Task Force also analyzes the efforts of eight leading social-networking sites to enhance the online safety of minors and makes recommendations concerning the best methods of ensuring the online safety of youth. The Task Force's literature review revealed that, although the risks facing youth online are complex, they are not significantly different from the risks facing youth offline. Moreover, the Task Force found that, as minors get older, they themselves contribute to the problem of online safety. Regarding the 40 technologies intended to enhance Internet safety, the Task Force recommends that caregivers and law enforcement agencies should carefully weigh the privacy and security issues associated with these technologies against their potential benefits.

Overall, the Task Force concludes that no single technological solution or specific combination of technological solutions can solve the problem of online safety for minors; rather, adults must employ these technologies in concert with other methods, including parental oversight, education, social services, and law enforcement. In addition, the Task Force recommends that social-networking sites and service providers should enact sound policies to protect minors from online predators.

McQuade, Samuel C., III, and Neel Sampat. "Survey of Internet and At-Risk Behaviors: Undertaken by School Districts of Monroe County, New York, May 2007 to June 2008 and October 2007 to January 2008." Report, Center for Multidisciplinary Studies, Rochester Institute of Technology, Rochester, New York, June 18, 2008.

In partnership with 14 school districts, the Rochester Institute of Technology (RIT) carried out a major study in 2007, which included an online survey of more than 40,000 students. The study measured the nature and extent of online experiences, as offender or as victim, of students in kindergarten through twelfth grade; determined levels and types of parental supervision over children's use of computers and portable electronic devices; and obtained information from teachers regarding their perceptions of school-related cyber abuse and crime. The surveys targeted students in developmentally distinct age and grade levels, as well as the parents of the students and the teachers and staff of their schools.

The results of the study indicate that children begin using the Internet at kindergarten age or younger and that online activities of children in grades K–1 2 include inappropriate behavior and exposure to inappropriate content. Cyberbullying and victimization begins as early as second grade for some children, and by middle school, students as a group experience or engage in all known forms of cyber abuse and online aggression. Online exchange of sexually explicit content typically begins in middle school. The study results also report that students consistently say that they are less supervised than their parents say that they are: 66 percent of high school students reported that their parents provide no supervision of Internet activities, but only 7 percent of parents reported that they do not provide any supervision.

Sabina, Chiara, Janis Wolak, and David Finkelhor. "Rapid Communication: The Nature and Dynamics of Internet Pornography Exposure for Youth." CyberPsychology and Behavior 11, no. 6 (2008): 691–93.

The article reports the results of a 2006 online survey in which researchers questioned a sample of college students about their exposure to online pornography before the age of 18, comparing the responses of male and female students. In the final sample of 563 students, 72.8 percent (93.2 percent of the male students and 62.1 percent of the female students) reported that they had viewed online pornography before the age of 18. Most initial exposure had occurred between the ages of 14 and 17, with boys significantly more likely to view pornography frequently and to view a variety of images and girls significantly more likely to expose themselves to pornography involuntarily. Specifically, 6.8 percent of males reported that they had never purposely sought exposure to pornography, whereas 42.3 percent of females reported that they had never looked for pornography on purpose. A small minority of the students reported that viewing online pornography before the age of 18 had strongly affected their attitudes or emotions about sexuality. Of this group, boys were more likely to report feeling excitement, whereas girls were more likely to experience embarrassment and disgust. However, the researchers found considerable diversity in the extent of and reactions to online pornography, and, therefore, suggested that relying on gender stereotypes might obscure the full picture of how youth respond to exposure.

Wells, Melissa, David Finkelhor, Janis Wolak, and Kimberly J. Mitchell. "Defining Child Pornography: Law Enforcement Dilemmas in Investigations of Internet Child Pornography Possession." Police Practice and Research 8, no. 3 (July 2007): 269–82.

The authors examine law enforcement agencies' difficulty defining child pornography, using a sample of 34 cases of reported possession of Internet child pornography in which law enforcement officers had made no arrest. Researchers analyzed data collected as part of the National Juvenile Online Victimization (NJOV) Study. NJOV sought to capture estimates of the incidence of Internet sex crimes against minors occurring during the course of one year (2000– 2001), which had come to the attention of law enforcement officials. In addition, NJOV attempted to identify problems in the investigations of those crimes. Analysts' findings reflected two dilemmas facing law enforcement agencies that can prevent their making an arrest in a child pornography case: 1) the nature of the child pornography portrayed in the confiscated images may not fit the definitions of existing statutes and 2) investigators may not be able to determine the age of the children in the images with certainty.

Wolak, Janis, Kimberly J. Mitchell, and David Finkelhor. "Unwanted and Wanted Exposure to Online Pornography in a National Sample of Youth Internet Users." Pediatrics 119, no. 2 (2007): 247–57.

The Crimes Against Children Research Center at the University of New Hampshire designed the Youth Internet Safety Survey to determine the incidence of and risk factors for youth exposure to sexual content on the Internet. In the Second Youth Internet Safety Survey, the researchers conducted a telephone survey between March and June 2005, interviewing a nationally representative sample of 1,500 youth Internet users ages 10 to 17. In this article, based on the analysis of the data from that survey, the researchers report the extent of both wanted and unwanted exposure to online pornography among regular Internet users in that age-group and assess associated risk factors. The researchers found that 42 percent of youth Internet users (approximately 600) had viewed online pornography during the previous year. Of that 42 percent, 66 percent of the youth (approximately 400) reported that they had not sought or desired the exposure to pornography. Thirty-four percent of youth Internet users viewing pornography online reported a mixture of intentional exposure only or both wanted and unwanted exposure during 2005, up from 25 percent during 1999 and 2000. The youth reported that unwanted exposure had occurred only during a single Internet activity—when they were using file-sharing programs to download images.

U.S. Congress. House of Representatives. Committee on Energy and Commerce. Subcommittee on Oversight and Investigations. "Sexual Exploitation of Children over the Internet." 109th Cong., 2d sess., January 2007. Staff Report. http://republicans.energycommerce.house.gove/1 08/News /0 1 032007_Report.pdf (accessed May 2009).

Prompted by Kurt Eichenwald's article, "Through His Webcam, a Boy Joins a Sordid Online World," which appeared in the New York Times at the end of 2005, the House Energy and Commerce Subcommittee on Oversight and Investigations studied the United States' efforts to curb the sexual exploitation of children over the Internet. Committee staff investigated the information Eichenwald had reported; visited federal law enforcement agency offices and conducted interviews; reviewed and analyzed existing federal law with regard to criminal penalties for possession, creation, and distribution of child pornography; and held hearings from April through September 2006.

The subcommittee reports that the ease of trading, selling, and downloading pornographic images of children from the Internet contributes to the increased incidence of sexual exploitation of children in the United States and the world. The number of sexually exploitative images of children on the Internet is increasing, and victims are typically younger and the images more violent than in the past. Commercially available child pornography on the Internet may comprise a multibillion-dollar-per-year industry. Although law enforcement agencies at the state level prosecute 70 percent of all cases involving sexual exploitation of children over the Internet, the subcommittee found a wide discrepancy among state criminal codes in their treatment of these offenses and in their sentencing practices. Investigators also reported that encryption methods, such as anonymizers, significantly interfere with law enforcement's ability to investigate and bring charges against offenders. The subcommittee also found that Web sites hosted in the United States appear to account for more than half of the child pornography on the Internet.

Malamuth, Neil, and Mark Huppin. "Drawing the Line on Virtual Child Pornography: Bringing the Law in Line with the Research Evidence." New York University Review of Law and Social Change 31 (2006–2007): 773–827.

This New York University law review article seeks to determine whether documented incidences of the use of various kinds of child pornography may be used as evidentiary material in child molestation cases. The authors used scientific literature to identify those individuals who might have a risk factor for perpetrating sexually abusive acts after exposure to virtual child pornography and attempted to assess the degree of risk such exposure might create for persons with this predisposition.

Drawing a clear distinction between pedophiles (individuals who are sexually aroused by children) and child molesters (individuals who commit sexual acts against children), the authors reviewed various case studies and found that, whereas child molesters use pornography to groom potential victims, as well as to self-stimulate before committing a sex crime against a child, pedophiles are less likely to molest a child after viewing pornography. A minority reported that pedophiles are more likely to molest a child after viewing pornography. The authors also analyzed scientific literature on aggression and on pornography that portrays nonconsenting adults, attempting to draw links among risk factors, exposure to child pornography, and the likelihood of a person committing a contact crime against a child. The authors conclude that whether exposure to real or virtual child pornography affects a person's behavior depends on a number of risk factors, and that, therefore, no strong causal relationship exists between viewing child pornography and committing sexual molestation of a child.

Cho, Chang-Hoan, and Hongsik John Cheon. "Children's Exposure to Negative Internet Content: Effects of Family Context." Journal of Broadcasting and Electronic Media 49, no. 4 (December 2005). *http://findarticles.com/p/articles/mi_m6836/is_4_49/ai_n25120984/* (accessed May 2009).

The article reports the results of an extensive review of the literature and a survey of 190 families, which the researchers conducted to study the extent of children's exposure to negative Internet content including pornography, violence, and sexual solicitation. The researchers simultaneously examined the discrepancy between parents' perception of their children's Internet use and their children's actual activities. The primary focus of this study was the social context of children's Internet use, particularly the relationship of their Internet use to family dynamics. The researchers believe that, rather than merely reporting the children's visits to Web sites or their general online activities, this study contributes new data concerning the content that children actually encounter on the Internet. In addition, the study provides new information regarding the role that the family environment and parent–child relationship play in a child's exposure to negative Internet content. Moreover, the authors believe that their research contributes a theoretical framework that encompasses both the incidence of children's negative exposure online and parents' perceived control over their children's Internet activities.

The researchers found that parents generally underestimate their children's exposure to negative material on the Internet. They suggest that, in fact, children encounter negative content more frequently than their parents believe. The study agrees with research conducted prior to 1995 that examined the effects of family communication patterns on children's use of mass media—finding that as with earlier studies, parents of families exhibiting high levels of cohesion perceive greater control over and understanding of their children's Internet use.

Ybarra, Michele L., and Kimberly J. Mitchell. "Exposure to Internet Pornography among Children and Adolescents: A National Survey." CyberPsychology and Behavior 8, no. 5 (2005): 473–86.

Analyzing data from the First Youth Internet Safety Survey (2000), which the Crimes Against Children Research Center at the University of New Hampshire designed to determine the incidence of and risk factors for youth exposure to sexual content on the Internet, this study focuses on youth who intentionally seek pornography. The authors found that the majority of youth who reported seeking pornography online and offline were male; only 5 percent of females reported having looked for pornography. The majority (87 percent) of those who reported having sought sexual images online were older than 14. The authors of the study noted the developmental appropriateness of this curiosity about sexuality in youth over the age of 14. The survey measured the following: pornography seeking, demographic characteristics, Internet-usage characteristics, unwanted exposure to sexual material, parental Internet controls, caregiver–child relationships, and psychosocial characteristics. The authors found that, although the majority of youth intentionally seeking pornography online are older than 14, younger children reported exposure to sexual images in magazines or on television. The younger children who were regular Internet users and who reported that they had intentionally sought pornography also reported a significantly higher incidence of delinquent behavior, substance use, or clinical depression, or a combination of these.

Analysis of the data identified several areas warranting further research: the small group of females intentionally seeking pornography; the link between purposeful exposure to pornography and emotional challenges, such as major depression or a poor emotional bond with a caregiver; the role of alcohol in delinquent behavior involving intentional seeking of pornography; and whether or not the Internet has become a more common mode of intentional exposure to pornography among adolescents than the viewing of sexually explicit material offline.

Cameron, Kenzie A., and Laura F. Salazar. "Adolescents' Experience with Sex on the Web: Results from Online Focus Groups." Journal of Adolescence 28, no. 4 (2005): 535–40.

This study fills a gap in the data on the effects of online sexualized material on children and adolescents. The researchers recruited 40 adolescents 1 8 male and 22 female ages 14 to 17 (in grades 9–1 1), who regularly used the Internet. The researchers divided the participants according to their age and gender into one of four Web-based focus groups. The focus-group interface among the participants in each group was similar to that in an online chat room, in which the participants are typically anonymous.

Focus-group participants reported having intentionally sought exposure to sexually oriented Web sites while searching for information related to sexual health or relationships. They reported having experienced unintentional exposure through personal e-mail with benign subject lines or when following misleading URLs. The participants reported an incidence of exposure to sexually explicit Web sites ranging from "never" to "daily," with most exposures occurring accidentally or unintentionally, via unsolicited e-mails containing explicit content or links to explicit material. Some participants reported having received 10 to 20 such e-mails per day. Most girls responded negatively to their exposure to sexually explicit material, and no girls reported intentional exposure. A subgroup of boys reported intentional exposure, whereas some reported that they had not sought to view the sexual content, stating that they considered explicit material "sick." Both boys and girls reported their perception that exposure to sexually explicit material had no effect on their personal views of either gender or of relationships. The authors of the study suggested further research in this area, noting that this perception contradicts previous research documenting the negative effects of adolescents' exposure to sexually explicit content.

Cooper, Sharon, Richard J. Estes, Angelo P. Giardino, Nancy D. Kellog, and Victor I. Vieth, eds. Medical, Legal, and Social Science Aspects of Child Sexual Exploitation: A Comprehensive Review of Pornography, Prostitution, and Internet Crimes. 2 vols. St. Louis, MO: G.W. Medical Publishing, 2005.

This two-volume set provides a repository of information for multidisciplinary teams studying Internet crimes against children. Volume 1 offers an overview of the scope of the problem of sexual exploitation of children, covering the subjects of pornography and online solicitation. Survivors, including prostituted children and youth, report their experiences. Chapters in volume 1 discuss abusive images of children on the Internet, the commercial sexual exploitation of children in North America, methods Internet predators use to exploit children sexually, and young people's remarks about online victimization. Volume 2 addresses the investigation and prosecution of Internet crimes against children and makes recommendations on how to prevent the exploitation of children. Topics in volume 2 include important actors in the investigation process, such as the U.S. Postal Inspection Service and first responders; the investigation process itself; issues concerning prosecution of purveyors of child pornography; the criminal justice system –including perspectives of victims, juvenile courts, and judges; pedophiles' activities on the Internet; and computer forensic software.

Greenfield, Patricia M. "Inadvertent Exposure to Pornography on the Internet: Implications of Peer-to-Peer File-Sharing Networks for Child

Development and Families." Applied Developmental Psychology 25 (2004): 741–50.

In this article, Patricia M. Greenfield of the Children's Medical Center and the Department of Psychology of the University of California at Los Angeles reports her March 13, 2003, testimony before the House Committee on Government Reform regarding the risk of children's and adolescents' unintended exposure to pornography through peer-to-peer file-sharing networks. In her testimony, Greenfield responded to the committee's questions concerning the developmental effects on children of exposure to pornography through file-sharing networks; the challenges parents face in limiting children's access to pornography online; and nontechnical tools available to parents that can help them address these challenges.

Greenfield provided overviews of various research studies and their findings. She concluded that evidence supports the thesis that pornography and sexualized material can influence the moral values, sexual activity, and sexual attitudes of children and youth, including their attitudes toward sexual violence; that peer-to-peer file-sharing networks are part of a pervasive, sexualized media environment that leads to inadvertent exposure of children and youth to pornography and other adult sexual content; and that a warm, communicative parent–child relationship, appropriate sex education, and parental participation in children's Internet activities are critical factors in protecting children from adverse effects of exposure to explicit sexual material. Greenfield also stated that parents of boys at risk for antisocial behavior should monitor their sons' Internet use carefully and limit their access to online pornography.

Mitchell, Kimberly J., David Finkelhor, and Janis Wolak. "Victimization of Youths on the Internet." Journal of Aggression, Maltreatment and Trauma 8, nos. 1–2 (May 2003): 1–3 9.

The Crimes Against Children Research Center at the University of New Hampshire designed the Youth Internet Safety Survey to determine the incidence of and risk factors for youth exposure to sexual content on the Internet. The First Youth Internet Safety Survey (2000) surveyed a nationally representative sample of 1,500 youth, examining the dangers that children and adolescents face when communicating, gathering information, or seeking entertainment on the Internet. The survey asked participants about unwanted sexual solicitations, unwanted exposure to sexual material, and online harassment during the previous year. In this article, researchers report their analysis of data from the survey.

The authors found that predators had targeted girls for sexual solicitation at almost twice the rate of boys, and youth who were at least 15 years old accounted for nearly two-thirds of incidents of unwanted exposure. In instances of harassment, predators had targeted boys and girls equally. The survey revealed that adults were responsible for 24 percent of solicitations—most of those adults were ages 18 to 25; only 4 percent of those soliciting were older than 25. Juveniles accounted for nearly half of all those targeted and for half of all aggressive solicitations. Harassment caused the young people the most distress—they described 31 percent of the instances of harassment as extremely upsetting, while 20 percent reported extremely upsetting solicitations, and 23 percent of youth felt extremely upset when exposed to sexual material. The authors found that young people at risk for unwanted solicitation, harassment, and exposure to sexual content on the Internet tend to be troubled, older adolescents who use the Internet frequently and engage in high-risk online behavior. However, they also found that half of the youth reporting unwanted solicitation, harassment, or exposure to sexual materials were not troubled, high-rate Internet users or frequent online risk takers.

Mitchell, Kimberly J., David Finkelhor, and Janis Wolak. "The Exposure of Youth to Unwanted Sexual Material on the Internet: A National Survey of Risk, Impact, and Prevention." Youth and Society 34, no. 3 (March 2003): 330–58.

Analyzing data from the First Youth Internet Safety Survey (2000), which the Crimes Against Children Research Center at the University of New Hampshire designed to determine the incidence of and risk factors for youth exposure to sexual material on the Internet, the researchers sought to identify a subset of unwanted exposure described as very or extremely distressing. Twenty-four percent of the 1,500 youth surveyed in this nationally representative sample reported feeling very or extremely upset about exposure to sexually explicit material, 21 percent reported feeling very or extremely embarrassed, and 19 percent reported experiencing at least one stress symptom related to the episode. Youth reporting symptoms of stress said that they had stayed away from the Internet after the incident, could not stop thinking about the episode, felt jumpy or irritable, or had lost interest in their usual pursuits. In 43 percent of the episodes, the youth had not disclosed their exposure to anybody. Those that did report it usually told a parent, friend, or sibling. When the youth or their family reported the incident to an authority, they most frequently told a teacher or school official or the Internet service provider, but they had never reported the incident to police.

The authors of the study discussed the survey's flaws, such as the lack of standardized, validated procedures for collecting data on children exposed to sexual material on the Internet. They conclude that the study indicates the urgent need to collect further evidence to inform public policy aimed at protecting youth from unsought exposure to sexually explicit material on the Internet.

U. S. General Accounting Office. "File-Sharing Programs: Peer-to-Peer Networks Provide Ready Access to Child Pornography." Report to the Chairman and Ranking Minority Member, Committee on Government Reform, House of Representatives, no. GAO–03–351, Washington, DC, 2003.

The U.S. General Accounting Office (GAO) produced this report in response to a request from the House Committee on Government Reform that GAO investigate the ease of access to child pornography on peer-to-peer networks; the risk of inadvertent exposure of juvenile users of peerto-peer networks to pornography (including child pornography); and the extent of federal law enforcement resources for combating child pornography on peer-to-peer networks. Agents at the Customs Cyber-Smuggling Center performed searches, and GAO performed analyses based on keywords and file names only, finding that child pornography is easily found and downloaded from peer-to-peer networks. Depending on the keywords used, child pornography comprised between 42 and 44 percent of pornographic images found in a search of KaZaA (a popular peerto-peer, file-sharing program). The results were consistent with the observations of the National Center for Missing & Exploited Children. Agents classified nearly half of the images downloaded from keyword searches using celebrity names and cartoon characters as pornography, indicating that youth face a significant risk of inadvertent exposure to pornography while using networks like KaZaA. GAO also analyzed data on the allocation of resources at four agencies, as well as resources that the National Center for Missing & Exploited Children had allocated to combat child pornography. GAO found that these agencies had not devoted significant resources to combating child exploitation and child pornography in 2003. GAO was unable to quantify the resources dedicated to child pornography investigations involving peer-topeer networks.

Thornburgh, Dick, and Herbert S. Lin, eds. Youth, Pornography and the Internet. Washington, DC: National Academy Press, 2002.

This 450-page volume (including a bibliography and an index) is the product of a 1998 mandate of the U.S. Congress charging the National Research Council (NRC) to carry out a study of pornography on the Internet.

In response, the NRC Computer Science and Telecommunications Board and the NRC Board on Children, Youth, and Families formed a committee to conduct the study. The committee members comprised a diverse group of people with expertise in constitutional law, law enforcement, libraries and library science, developmental and social psychology, information technologies, ethics, and education. Chapters in this volume cover relevant technologies, such as filtering, age verification software, and anonymizers; the adult online entertainment industry and its practices related to minors; legal and regulatory issues, particularly issues related to the First Amendment, to federal and state laws and regulatory efforts, and to law enforcement; children's exposure to sexually explicit material on the Internet; research concerning the effects on individuals of exposure to sexually explicit material; public debate concerning the effects of such exposure; and legal and regulatory tools for protecting children from obscene material on the Internet.

Jenkins, Philip. Beyond Tolerance: Child Pornography on the Internet. New York: New York University Press, 2001.

Over the course of nine chapters, Jenkins, a professor of history and religion who has written extensively about public perceptions of social problems, examines the issue of Internet regulation through the lens of child pornography. In the unique case of child pornography, Jenkins concludes that the government should impose some form of regulation aimed at drastically reducing the presence of child pornography on the Internet. However, he acknowledges the persistent difficulty of determining what law or laws might successfully achieve this end. Jenkins advocates the transformation of present law enforcement tactics and priorities to meet the goal of controlling child pornography. He explores society's views of child pornography and examines the new form of technology-driven social organization, which he considers responsible for perpetuating the problem of online child pornography.

In his discussion of the social context of online pornography, Jenkins provides an overview of the history of child pornography on the Internet and explains how the business of online child pornography developed, how it became highly organized and globalized, and why law enforcement officers have such difficulty identifying the participants. He examines the myths and realities of child pornography and discusses efforts to eradicate it, including debates about trade regulations, users' privacy, and individual rights; the official endeavors of law enforcement agencies; and the work of private activist groups.

Unwanted Sexual Solicitation

Dombrowski, Stefan C., Karen L. Gischlar, and Theo Durst. "Safeguarding Young People from Cyber Pornography and Cyber Sexual Predation: A Major Dilemma of the Internet." Child Abuse Review 16, no. 3 (2007): 153–70.

This article outlines technological and psychoeducational mechanisms to help caregivers parents or guardians protect children from online pornography and sexual solicitation. With the increased use of Internet technologies, such as e-mail, chat rooms, and peer-to-peer networks, children can easily connect with other people online at all times. Without caregiver supervision and interdiction of online communication, youth are vulnerable to exposure to pornography or to the solicitations of predators. However, the combination of technological methods and the vigilance of caregivers can deter solicitation and protect children from exposure to online pornography, safeguarding their emotional health. Software tools such as firewall security barriers, wireless encryption, antivirus protection, spyware detection and removal, and usage tracking help protect youth from accessing unsafe Web sites and allow the caregiver to review the child's online activity. However, although technological protections may stop some, determined predators can circumvent most of these methods. Therefore, caregivers also need to use psychoeducational measures, tailored to the child's developmental level, setting appropriate boundaries for online behavior.

Caregivers should discuss Internet dangers, supervise Internet friendships, monitor children's Internet use, and establish an Internet-use safety contract with the child. The article includes a sample Internet-use contract for the use of caregivers and their children. The authors prescribe a combination of technology-based tools and caregiver vigilance as the best way to defend children from solicitation and pornography.

Mitchell, Kimberly J., David Finkelhor, and Janis Wolak. "Online Requests for Sexual Pictures from Youth: Risk Factors and Incident Characteristics." Journal of Adolescent Health 41, no. 2 (2007): 196–203. http://www.unh.edu/ccrc/pdf/CV155.pdf (accessed March 27, 2009).

This study is based on data from the Second Youth Internet Safety Survey conducted between March and June 2005, in which researchers conducted telephone interviews with a nationally representative sample of 1,500 youth Internet users ages 10 to 17. The Crimes Against Children Research Center at the University of New Hampshire created the survey to examine youth exposure to sexual content on the Internet. The authors focus on one way that the Internet facilitates the production of child pornography: the solicitation of youth to produce sexually explicit images and to post or to transmit them online.

Reporting the demographic, psychological, and Internet-use characteristics of youth who received online solicitations for sexual pictures within the previous year, the authors found that 13 percent of youth in the study population had received unwanted sexual solicitations over the Internet, and 4 percent of the youth had received an online request to send a sexual picture of themselves. Only one youth out of the 65 who received such a request complied. Of the 1,500 survey respondents, 20 percent (300 youth) reported that they had received unwanted sexual solicitations or harassment, and 45 percent of those solicitations (136 youth 13 percent of the overall survey group) included requests for pictures. Forty-eight percent (65 youth) had received requests for sexual images. The survey found that youth who are female, black, in the presence of friends, have close online relationships, or engage in online sexual behavior are more likely than others to receive solicitations for sexual pictures. The study defined online relationships as relationships with peers and nonsexual relationships with adults, defining online sexual behavior as talking about sex online with someone the youth does not know personally. The authors call for pediatric and adolescent health professionals to be aware of the incidence of online requests for sexual pictures of youth and of the Internet's role in expanding the production of child pornography.

Mitchell, Kimberly J., Janis Wolak, and David Finkelhor. "Trends in Youth Reports of Sexual Solicitations, Harassment and Unwanted Exposure to Pornography on the Internet." Journal of Adolescent Health 40, no. 2 (2007): 116–26. http://www.unh.edu/ccrc/pdf/ CV135.pdf (accessed March 24, 2009).

This 2007 report compares the results of two surveys, designed by the Crimes Against Children Research Center at the University of New Hampshire and conducted in 2000 and 2005, regarding unwanted sexual solicitation, harassment, and exposure to pornography on the Internet. In the First and Second Youth Internet Safety Surveys, researchers conducted telephone interviews with a nationally representative sample of youth Internet users ages 10 to 17. This article differentiates the results of the two surveys according to demographic characteristics, such as age, gender, race, and household income, revealing changes that occurred between 2000 and 2005. The surveys defined unwanted sexual solicitations as requests to engage in sexual activities or sexual talk, or as adults' requests for sexual information from a juvenile; they defined online harassment as threats or other aggressive behavior toward a youth, sent or posted online; and they defined unwanted exposure to pornography as unsought and unexpected exposure to pictures of naked people or of people having sex.

In general, the results of the two surveys indicated that, although unwanted sexual solicitations had declined, online harassment and unwanted exposure to pornography had increased between 2000 and 2005. Unwanted sexual solicitations had decreased, overall, from 19 percent to 13 percent. The decline in such activity was most apparent among white youth living in affluent areas. However, the incidence of online harassment had risen from 6 percent to 9 percent overall, and the incidence of unwanted exposure to pornography had risen from 25 percent to 34 percent. Demographic subgroups showed different results for the incidence of sexual solicitation and unwanted exposure to pornography. For example, the 2005 survey showed that black youth and low-income families had experienced an increased incidence of sexual solicitation. Unwanted exposure to pornography had increased among youth 10 to 12 years old, 16- to 17-year olds, boys, and white, non-Hispanic youth. The authors observe that, despite the decline in certain types of Internet crimes against children, young people continue to experience offensive episodes online. Caregivers, social service providers, and law enforcement agents need to target minority and less affluent populations for prevention programs, to protect them from online harassment and from predators.

Mitchell, Kimberly J., Janis Wolak, and David Finkelhor. "Police Posing as Juveniles Online to Catch Sex Offenders: Is It Working?" Sexual Abuse: A Journal of Research and Treatment 17, no. 3 (July 2005): 241–67. http://www.unh.edu/ccrc/pdf/CV82.pdf (accessed March 28, 2009).

The article explores the extent and effectiveness of proactive online investigations, in which police investigators use the Internet posing as minors and often assuming a different gender to communicate via chat rooms, e-mail, and instant messaging, to interdict youth enticement and child pornography. The authors used data from the National Juvenile Online Victimization Study (NJOV), which reported characteristics of Internet sex crimes against minors, to create a survey for law enforcement agencies. The survey of 2,574 state, county, and local law enforcement agencies found that, through proactive investigations, the agencies had made 124 arrests for Internet sex crimes against children during the year beginning July 1, 2000, and ending June 30, 2001.

The authors found that a significant proportion–25 percent–of all arrests for Internet crimes against children were the outcome of proactive investigations. Proactive investigations resulted in offenders entering pleas 91 percent of the time and going to trial 15 percent of the time (some offenders had multiple charges, accounting for the discrepancy in the percentages). Investigators most frequently posed as girls of 12 years old or older, meeting targeted predators in chat rooms or through instant messaging. In 87 percent of the cases, investigators conducted their investigations using multiple forms of online communication. The authors point out that, in 63 percent of the cases reviewed, the law enforcement agency had received no federal funding for this kind of investigative work. They conclude that, because of the high rate of arrest and the potential to stop a perpetrator before a child is molested, law enforcement agencies should continue to conduct proactive investigations.

Wolak, Janis, David Finkelhor, and Kimberly J. Mitchell. "Internet-Initiated Sex Crimes Against Minors: Implications for Prevention Based on Findings from a National Study." Journal of Adolescent Health 35, no. 5 (2004): 11–20. http://www.unh.edu/ccrc/pdf/CV71.pdf (accessed March 23, 2009).

This article describes characteristics of interactions between Internet predators and their juvenile victims. Survey results revealed that the majority of victims had met the predator willingly. In a mailed survey and follow-up telephone interview with law enforcement investigators, conducted between October 2001 and July 2002, researchers identified 129 Internet-initiated sex crimes. The cases involved sex-crime victims, ages 17 and younger, who had first met the predator on the Internet. Face-to-face meetings had occurred in 74 percent of the cases, and 93 percent of those encounters had included sexual contact. Most of the victims (73 percent) met with the predators more than once. The majority of victims (67 percent) were children between the ages of 12 and 15, and 75 percent of the victims were girls. The most common first encounter of a predator with a victim took place in an online chat room (76 percent). In 47 percent of the cases, the predator offered gifts or money during the relationship-building phase.

This study found that two widely held beliefs regarding online predation were incorrect. First, the researchers found that predators use less deception to befriend their online victims than experts had thought. Only 5 percent of the predators told their victims that they were in the same age-group as the victim. Most offenders told the victim that they were older males seeking sexual relations. Second, a large majority of the victims who responded to this survey had willingly met and had sexual encounters with the predators. Internet victim-prevention programs have emphasized the dangers of predator deception, but, thus far, educators have not addressed the problems of youth who are willing to meet with adults to have voluntary sexual relationships. The authors conclude that vulnerable youth need further education regarding the negative effects of such relationships.

Berson, Ilene R. "Grooming Cybervictims: The Psychological Effects of Online Exploitation for Youth." Journal of School Violence 2, no. 1 (2003): 9–18. http://www.cs.auckland.ac.nz/ ~john/NetSafe/I.Berson.pdf (accessed March 20, 2009).

This article describes how online predators prepare potential child victims for abuse. The Internet poses a challenge for young users, because children's naïveté and trust make them vulnerable targets for predators seeking to groom them for illicit activities. In addition, the Internet permits anonymity, enabling the predator to hide his or her age and gender from the victim. Victims are often too young to interpret cues that would make an older person cautious.

Predators manipulate their victims through a process known as grooming, using techniques to lower the child's inhibitions and build his or her trust in the predator. Young people share personal information in chat rooms or in e-mail, not realizing that predators use such information to develop victim profiles, build an online friendship, and gain trust. The predator preys upon a child's loneliness and emotional neediness, gradually increasing the intensity of the interaction with the child by offering attention, friendship, and gifts. After building the child's trust, the perpetrator may gradually expose the child to pornography to lower the child's inhibitions, desensitize the child to nudity, and validate adult–child sexual relations. Finally, the perpetrator requests a personal meeting with the victim. Parents, schools, and government agencies need to foster awareness of online exploitation, explain to children the lures that predators offer them, and teach them to discriminate among types of online interactions, including ambiguous chat or e-mail content and potentially threatening exchanges.

Brown, Duncan. "Developing Strategies for Collecting and Presenting Grooming Evidence in a High Tech World." Update (National Center for Prosecution of Child Abuse), 2001, 1. http:www.ndaa. org/publications /newsletters/update_volume_1 4_number_1 1_200 1 .html (accessed March 24, 2009).

In this unique article, a guide for prosecutors seeking to prosecute online predators, the author describes the process that online predators use to prepare children for sexual exploitation, a process known as grooming, explaining the type of evidence against predators that law enforcement officers need to acquire and how to present the evidence at trial. The online predator follows the same grooming process as predators who do not use the Internet. First, the predator meets the child and builds trust through deception. Once the child develops trust in the perpetrator, the perpetrator often exposes the child to pornography to lower the child's inhibitions about sex. The Internet offers perpetrators the opportunity to groom multiple victims at the same time, because the technology allows perpetrators to communicate with potential victims without drawing public attention to themselves. The perpetrator may use photographic or other electronic equipment to capture and transmit images of the victim. Law enforcement officers must acquire probative evidence against the perpetrator, collecting and preserving all evidence of grooming, such as pornography, Web cameras, and other electronic equipment, so that prosecutors can present the evidence at trial to show the perpetrator's motivation.

The author describes the online grooming process, details evidence, and shows how to use the evidence in trial. Understanding the typical procedure that online predators follow when committing an offense enables prosecutors to use evidence of the process to build a solid case against online predators.

HARASSMENT

Chaffin, Stacy M. "The New Playground Bullies of Cyberspace: Online Peer Sexual Harassment." Howard Law Journal 51, no. 3 (2008): 777–818.

Focusing on online sexual harassment among adolescent peers, the author of this study reviews legal cases that limit students' freedom of speech. Online peer sexual harassment occurs among teenagers when schoolmates, classmates, and friends use e-mail, cell phones, text messaging, instant messaging, personal Web sites, social-networking Web sites, and polling Web sites to make threats against and spread sexual rumors about their adolescent peers. The author argues that, although school administrators are already taking steps to prohibit offline sexual harassment, they also need to prevent online sexual harassment. In support of her call for action, Chaffin cites stories of children who have taken their own lives after experiencing online sexual harassment. Middle school and high school children form online groups, behaving in hurtful ways, such as dehumanizing a classmate, behavior that they are less likely to engage in outside of the group. Both groups and individuals often use social-networking Web sites, such as Facebook, My Space, and YouTube, to harass their peers.

Court decisions regarding students' rights to free speech including Tinker v. Des Moines Independent Community School District, (1, below) which permits schools to discipline students for harmful speech; Bethel School District No. 403 v. Fraser, (2, below) which finds that students' expressive rights are not equal to those of adults; and Hazelwood School District v. Kuhlmeier, (3, below) which finds that schools need not tolerate students' speech if it impedes the school's basic educational mission —support the argument that online sexual harassment does not deserve protection under the First Amendment and that schools should regulate such behavior. Nevertheless, even though online sexual harassment is harmful to young people, most schools do not discipline students for engaging in it. The author believes that school administrators should treat online sexual harassment as a threat to adolescent safety and act to protect students from harassment.

1 *Tinker v. Des Moines Independent Community School District,* 393 U.S. 503 (1969).
2 *Bethel School District V. Fraser,* 478 U.S. 675, 678 (1986).
3 *Hazelwood School District v. Kuhlmeier,* 484 U.S. 260 (1988).

The National Campaign to Prevent Teen and Unwanted Pregnancy and CosmoGirl.com. "Sex and Tech: Results from a Survey of Teen and Young Adults." Report, Washington, DC, 2008. *http://www.thenationalcampaign.org/sextech/PDF/SexTech_Summary.pdf* accessed March 26, 2009).

This study presents the results, including the questionnaire and responses, of a unique survey on text messaging of sexual content among adolescents and young adults. Sexting is adolescent slang referring to the sending or receiving of sexually suggestive images and text messages, often by cell phone. Participants in the study -653 teenagers, ages 13 to 19, and 627 young adults, ages 20 to 26 completed the online survey between September 25, 2008, and October 3, 2008. The researchers further analyzed some of the survey responses according to gender or age for example, they segregated the responses of young adolescents ages 13 to 16. A considerable number of those 13 to 19 years old in this survey had sent, by electronic means, nude or seminude pictures or sexually suggestive text. Twenty percent of teenagers had sent nude or seminude pictures or videos of themselves, and 11 percent of girls ages 13 to 16 had sent such images. Thirty-nine percent of teenagers reported having sent sexually suggestive text messages, and 48 percent of teenagers reported having received such messages. Of those teenagers who had sent sexually suggestive content, 71 percent of the girls and 67 percent of the boys reported that they had sent the content to their boyfriends or girlfriends. However, 15 percent of those teenagers said that they had sent or posted nude or seminude pictures to people known to them only through online contact. Of those teenagers who had sent sexually suggestive content, 66 percent of the girls and 60 percent of the boys said that they had sent the material for fun or to flirt, and 12 percent of said that they had sent it because they felt pressured to send sexually suggestive messages or images. The study offers points for adolescents to consider before they send sexually suggestive content and suggestions to help parents speak with their children about sex and technology.

Lenhart, Amanda. "Cyberbullying and Online Teens." Research Memo, Pew/Internet and American Life Project, Pew Research Center, Washington, DC, June 27, 2007. http://www.pewinternet.org/~/media 20Memo.pdf.pdf (accessed March 23, 2009).

In the national Parents and Teens 2006 Survey, researchers conducted telephone interviews, from October 23, 2006, to November 19, 2006, of 935 youth Internet users ages 12 to 17. Based on the reports of youth identified as victims of cyberbullying in that survey, the author reports the prevalence and pattern of online harassment and bullying among adolescents. The study found that 32 percent of the teenagers interviewed had been harassed online. Girls especially older girls, ages 15 to 17 - were more likely to have experienced online harassment than boys: 38 percent of the girls and 41 percent of the older girls had experienced online harassment, as compared to 26 percent of the boys. Sending or forwarding a private e-mail was the most common method of cyberbullying (comprising 15 percent of all cyberbullying incidents), followed by spreading rumors online (13 percent), sending threatening or aggressive messages (13 percent), and posting an embarrassing picture (6 percent). Older teenage girls, ages 15 to 17, were most likely to receive online threats. Teenagers who provided personal information on a social-networking site were more likely to be the target of harassment (comprising 39 percent of social network users) than those who did not use a social-networking site (23 percent). Fewer than one in three teenagers (29 percent of those interviewed) said that online bullying is more common than offline bullying, but 33 percent of the girls interviewed reported that online bullying is more common.

Ybarra, Michele L., and Kimberly J. Mitchell. "Prevalence and Frequency of Internet Harassment Instigation: Implications for Adolescent Health." Journal of Adolescent Health 41, no. 2 (2007): 189–95. *http://www.unh.edu/ccrc/pdf/CV157.pdf* (accessed March 20, 2009).

The authors describe the pervasiveness of mental health problems among youth who harass others on the Internet. The study is based on data from the Second Youth Safety Internet Survey, which the Crimes Against Children Research Center at the University of New Hampshire designed to study youth exposure to sexual content, solicitation, and harassment on the Internet. Between March 2005 and June 2005, researchers conducted telephone interviews of a nationally representative sample of 1,500 youth ages 10 to 17 years old. The authors of this article analyzed the survey results to identify the frequency with which the youth engaged in harassment activity, categorizing the offenders as 1) limited harassers who had engaged in harassment one or two times in the past year, 2) occasional harassers who had engaged in harassment three to five times in the past year, and 3) frequent harassers who had engaged in harassment six or more times in the past year.

The survey indicated that youth with behavioral and psychological problems were more likely than others to engage in online harassment. Frequent harassers were seven times more likely to have rule-breaking problems and nine times more likely to have aggression problems than those who did not harass others online. Boys were three times more likely to be frequent harassers than girls. Of those youth who harassed other youth online, 82 percent had been harassed online by someone else. Survey results also indicated that almost 30 percent of youth had harassed others online during the past year: 6 percent of youth had frequently harassed others via the Internet; 6 percent had occasionally harassed others online; and 17 percent had harassed others a limited number of times in the previous year. Because harassment events increase as psychological or behavioral problems increase, the frequency with which a youth engages in online harassment may be an indicator that mental health professionals can use to identify young people with psychological and behavioral problems.

Ybarra, Michele L., and Kimberly J. Mitchell. "Youth Engaging in Online Harassment: Associations with Caregiver-Child Relationships, Internet Use, and Personal Characteristics." Journal of Adolescence 27, no 3 (2004): 3 19–36. http://www.unh.edu/ ccrc/pdf/jvq/CV63.pdf (accessed March 16, 2009).

This study examines psychosocial indicators present in preteen and teenage youth who use the Internet to harass their peers. The authors define Internet harassment as an intentional and overt act of aggression toward another person online, citing as examples, rude comments or intentional embarrassment. Researchers based this study on the First Youth Internet Safety Survey, conducted between September 1999 and February 2000. The Crimes Against Children Research Center at the University of New Hampshire designed the survey to study youth exposure to sexual content, solicitation, and harassment on the Internet. Researchers conducted telephone interviews with a nationally representative sample of 1,500 youth Internet users between the ages of 10 and 17.

Analyzing the results of the survey, the authors of this article attempted to determine whether online bullies differ from traditional, offline bullies. The study found differences and similarities between offline and online aggressors. Although boys commit most incidents of offline harassment, the number of boys and girls who use the Internet to harass their peers is almost equal. Both offline bullies and youth who harass others online often have multiple psychosocial issues: 51 percent of all bullies had been victims of traditional bullying, 44 percent had a poor relationship with their caregiver, 37 percent showed a pattern of delinquency, and 32 percent were frequent substance abusers. The authors suggest that mental-health practitioners, healthcare providers, and educators need to address the mental health issues of those who use the Internet to harass others, as well as the mental health issues of those who are victims of online harassment.

Roban, Whitney. "The Net Effect: Girls and New Media." Executive Summary, Girl Scout Research Institute, Girl Scouts of the United States of America, New York, 2002. *http://www.girlscouts.org/research/pdf/net_effect.pdf* (accessed March 20, 2009).

This article, reporting a 2001 study of 1,246 girls, examines how parents can help their 13- to 18-year-old daughters use the Internet safely. Unlike other studies on the topic of adolescent Internet use, this study focused on teenage girls only and used a variety of methodologies, including small-group interviews, journals, written surveys, and an online survey. The study revealed that, although girls in this age-group know a lot about computers and the Internet, they still need and desire adult guidance. Fifty-eight percent of the girls reported that they themselves were the most computer-savvy person in their households. This finding indicates that, more than likely, not all girls are receiving pertinent Internet-safety information from their parents. Most girls said that they use their common sense to behave safely on the Internet. A majority of the girls—75 percent—said that their parents had set Internet rules for them, but 57 percent reported that they had broken those rules. The girls reported that parental rules included time limits on Internet use and prohibitions against online chatting, online shopping, and online romances or face-to-face meetings. Girls had also received prohibitive directives from their parents, such as "Don't give out personal information." However, the study suggests that girls need proactive advice as well. The girls reported their perception that their parents are concerned about the wrong things, such as the type of information the girls can access online, the kind of people they might contact, and their online behavior. The girls expressed their desire for their parents to teach them responsibility, to educate them about possible dangers, and to trust them to use the Internet safely.

The study concluded that parents should try to be more proactive in their relationship with their daughters. By attempting to understand their daughters' online lives and by developing trusting relationships with them, parents can learn to communicate better with their daughters and help them navigate positive and negative Internet experiences.

Cyberbullying

Kowalski, Robin M. "Cyber Bullying: Recognizing and Treating Victim and Aggressor." Psychiatric Times 25, no. 11 (October 1, 2008): 45–47.

In this brief article, the author describes the course of treatment that mental-health professionals offer cyberbullies and their victims. The author defines cyberbullying as bullying by means of electronic communications, such as instant messaging, e-mail, chat rooms, and cell phones, and defines eight specific forms of cyberbullying, such as harassment and exclusion. Therapeutic treatment begins with the psychological assessment of both victim and bully. First, the psychotherapist addresses the victim's immediate psychological needs, such as treatment for depression and anxiety. The psychotherapist reassures the victim that the bullying is not his or her fault. The psychotherapist follows up by teaching the victim strategies for protecting and asserting himself or herself in the future. However, the therapist provides a different therapeutic treatment to a cyberbully. Bullies need to accept responsibility for what they have done and understand the cost of their actions. Therapists work with cyberbullies to help them develop empathy for the pain they have inflicted, so that they understand the consequences of their behavior.

The author reports common warning signs of cyberbullying, such as anxiety, depression, poor health, poor school performance, and social isolation. In addition, the author suggests the need for further research, including case studies of interventions with cyberbullies. Given the frequency of teenagers' use of technologies to connect with one another, mental health professionals need to be aware of the dangers of cyberbullying.

Kowalski, Robin M., and Susan P. Limber. "Electronic Bullying Among Middle School Students." Journal of Adolescent Health 41, no. 6 (2007): S22–S30. *http://www.wctlaw.com/CM/Custom/Electronic%20Bullying% 20 Among%20Middle%20School%* 20Students.pdf (accessed March 24, 2009).

For this study, which focuses on electronic bullying among middle school students, 1,852 boys and 1,915 girls in sixth-, seventh-, and eighth-grade classes in the southeastern and northwestern United States completed 3,767 questionnaires. The authors chose these grades for the study because of the prevalence of traditional, offline bullying during these school years and the growing use of electronic media by middle school students. The study defined electronic bullying as bullying that takes place through Internet chat rooms, e-mail, instant messaging, text messaging, or Web sites. Eleven percent of the students reported being electronically bullied one or more times in the previous two months; 7 percent stated that they had bullied others electronically and had been the victims of electronic bullying; and 4 percent reported that they had bullied others electronically but had not been victims. Fifteen percent of the girls were the victims of electronic bullying, as compared with 7 percent of the boys, and sixth-grade girls were half as likely as seventh- and eighth-grade girls to be the victims of electronic bullying. The percentage of girl victims rose with each grade level, while the percentage of boy victims declined from seventh to eighth grade. The percentage of girl bullies who were also victims rose with each grade level, with the percentage of boy bullies who also were victims declining between seventh and eighth grade. Middle school youth most often experienced electronic bullying via instant messaging (66 percent), followed by chat rooms (25 percent), e-mail (24 percent), Web sites (23 percent), and text messaging (14 percent). The authors conclude that electronic bullying is a significant problem, suggesting that one potential means of preventing it is for schools to enact rules and policies prohibiting electronic bullying, in addition to those already in place to prevent offline bullying.

Moessner, Chris. "Cyberbullying." Trends and Tudes, April 2007, 1–4. *http://www. harrisinteractive.com/news/newsletters/k12news/HI_ TrendsTudes_2007_v06_i04.pdf* (accessed March 23, 2009).

This study focuses on adolescents' reactions to cyberbullying. The National Crime Prevention Council commissioned this 2007 report by Harris Interactive, based on a national survey of 846 children ages 13 to 17. The council chose this age-group because parents tend to give children in this population less supervision than at other ages. The study defines cyberbullying as the use of the Internet, cell phones, or other technology to send or to post text or images intended to hurt or embarrass another person.The researchers asked young people about the prevalence of cyberbullying and their responses to it. More than four in 10 teenagers (43 percent) in this survey reported that they had experienced cyberbullying in the previous year, with the most common occurrence among those 15 and 16 years old. Although many middle school students (48 percent) and high school students (58 percent) reported that cyberbullying did not bother them, 58 percent of middle school students and 56 percent of high school students commonly responded to cyberbullying with anger. Girls (63 percent) reacted with anger more often than boys (48 percent). Seventy-one percent of teenagers surveyed believe that the most effective means of preventing cyberbullying is software that blocks site access, and 62 percent think that refusing to forward cyberbully messages is most effective.

Unique to this survey was a question about the school administration's role in preventing cyberbullying: only 33 percent of the teenagers felt schools should educate students about cyberbullying. However, 37 percent agreed that schools should have rules prohibiting cyberbullying. The study suggests that parents can help their children avoid cyberbullies by setting expectations for online behavior and monitoring their children's Internet activities.

Patchin, Justin W., and Sameer Hinduja. "Bullies Move Beyond the Schoolyard: A Preliminary Look at Cyberbullying." Youth Violence and Juvenile Justice 4, no. 2 (April 2006): 148–69.

In this preliminary look at the issue of cyberbullying, the authors describe the negative impact online bullying has on youth, providing the results of a survey conducted to determine the extent and nature of online bullying. The article defines cyberbullying as willful and repeated harm inflicted through the medium of electronic text. Cyberbullying causes public humiliation and embarrassment, which can lead to serious psychological, emotional, and social wounds. Adolescents' online interaction their cyber life often revolves around school. Events occurring at school are often the topic of cyber conversation, and cyber conversations often continue at school. The interaction between adolescents' school and cyber life has the potential to cause victims of cyberbullying greater public embarrassment than traditional, offline bullying.

To show the prevalence of cyberbullying among teenagers, the authors linked their Internet- based survey, conducted between May 1, 2004, and May 31, 2004, to a popular musician's Web site, and the vast majority of respondents were female. Therefore, the survey results may not apply to other populations. More than 47 percent of the 384 teenagers reported that they had observed online bullying, almost 30 percent reported having been bullied online, and 11 percent reported that they had bullied others online. The most common form of cyberbullying was to ignore someone online (accounting for 60 percent of cyberbullying incidents), followed by disrespecting someone (50 percent), calling someone names (30 percent), and threatening someone (21 percent). Telling the online bully to stop was the most common adolescent response (36 percent). The authors suggest that cyberbullying merits further academic inquiry to determine whether cyberbullies or their victims are at risk for future deviant behavior.

Strom, Paris S., and Robert D. Strom. "Cyberbullying by Adolescents: A Preliminary Assessment." Educational Forum 70, no. 1 (Fall 2005): 21–36.

This study, which examines cyberbullying in general, is unique in pointing out that cyberbullies threaten students and school staff and in describing steps that schools can take to repel this threat. The authors report an incident in which a student wrote about his hatred for a particular teacher on a Web site, commenting that neither students nor school staff feels safe when the community permits teenagers to cyberbully.

The authors suggest a number of ways for parents and school staff to minimize cyberbullying, including educational programs and improved communication with teenagers. The article reports that state departments of education are creating programs to educate teachers and school administrators about the problem of cyberbullying. The authors propose that, in addition, information technology staff in the school districts could design and deliver curriculum to educate students, teachers, and parents about appropriate cyber conduct and how to respond to online persecution. Schools could poll their students to determine whether they have experienced cyberbullying and what the extent of cyberbullying is in the school community. Adults, who generally use technology only as a tool, need to understand that adolescents consider technology, such as computers, text messaging, and chat rooms, an essential part of their social life. Parents need to develop close communication with their children, encouraging their teenagers to tell them if somebody bullies them online. Parents and adolescents need to report cases of cyberbullying to the police. Finally, the authors propose the need for new studies to determine methods of confronting and preventing cyberbullying.

Annotated Bibliography: Child Pornography and Contact Offending

This annotated bibliography was prepared by the National Criminal Justice Resource Center in September, 2009. The search was conducted in the professional, peer reviewed literature in psychology, criminology, victim-mology, child development, and sociology published between 2000 and 2009.

Understanding Online Child Pornography Use: Applying Sexual Offense Theory to Internet Offenders

Elliott, Ian A.; Beech, Anthony R.

Aggression and Violent Behavior, May2009, Vol. 14 Issue 3, p180-193, 14p. Abstract: This review outlines the links between contemporary etiological and offense-process theories of child sexual abuse and our current knowledge of individuals who commit offenses related to online child pornography. First, we integrate previous behavioral typologies into a four-category internet offender typology. Second, we summarize development of etiological theory and evaluate the strengths and weaknesses of these theories in explaining the child pornography offender. Third, we outline the potential situational and ecological factors relating to the online environment that may also be a cause for the development and maintenance of prurient online behavior. Fourth, we review theories of the offense process and apply these to research into the modus operandi of child pornography offenders. Finally, we examine the usefulness of this approach in the assessment of risk and the treatment of online offenders.

The 'Butner Study' Redux: A Report of the Incidence of Hands-on Child Victimization by Child Pornography Offenders.

Bourke, Michael L.; Hernandez, Andres E.

Journal of Family Violence, vol. 24, no. 3, pp. 183-191, Apr 2009. Abstract: This study compared two groups of child pornography offenders participating in a voluntary treatment program: men whose known sexual offense history at the time of judicial sentencing involved the possession, receipt, or distribution of child abuse images, but did not include any 'hands-on' sexual abuse; and men convicted of similar offenses who had documented histories of hands-on sexual offending against at least one child victim. The goal was to determine whether the former group of offenders were 'merely' collectors of child pornography at little risk for engaging in hands-on sexual offenses, or if they were contact sex offenders whose criminal sexual behavior involving children, with the exception of Internet crimes, went undetected. Our findings show that the Internet offenders in our sample were significantly more likely than not to have sexually abused a child via a hands-on act. They also indicate that the offenders who abused children were likely to have offended against multiple victims, and that the incidence of 'crossover' by gender and age is high.

The Consumption of Internet Child Pornography and Violent and Sex Offending.

Endrass J, Urbaniok F, Hammermeister LC, Benz C, Elbert T, Laubacher A, Rossegger A. BMC Psychiatry, 2009; Vol. 9, pp. 43.

Abstract: BACKGROUND: There is an ongoing debate on whether consumers of child pornography pose a risk for hands-on sex offenses. Up until now, there have been very few studies which have analyzed the association between the consumption of child pornography and the subsequent perpetration of hands-on sex offenses. The aim of this study was to examine the recidivism rates for hands-on and hands-off sex offenses in a sample of child pornography users using a 6 year follow-up design. METHODS: The current study population consisted of 231 men, who were subsequently charged with consumption of illegal pornographic material after being detected by a special operation against Internet child pornography, conducted by the Swiss police in 2002. Criminal history, as well as recidivism, was assessed using the criminal records from 2008. RESULTS: 4.8% (n = 11) of the study sample had a prior conviction for a sexual and/or violent offense, 1% (n = 2) for a hands-on sex offense, involving child sexual abuse, 3.3% (n = 8) for a hands-off sex offense and one for a nonsexual violent offense. When applying a broad definition of recidivism, which included ongoing investigations, charges and convictions, 3% (n = 7) of the study sample recidivated with a violent and/or sex offense, 3.9% (n = 9) with a hands-off sex offense and 0.8% (n = 2) with a hands-on sex offense. CONCLUSION: Consuming child pornography alone is not a risk factor for committing hands-on sex offenses - at least not for those subjects who had never committed a hands-on sex offense. The majority of the investigated consumers had no previous convictions for hands-on sex offenses. For those offenders, the prognosis for hands-on sex offenses, as well as for recidivism with child pornography, is favorable.

Pedophiles in Wonderland: Censoring the Sinful in Cyberspace.

Russell, Gabrielle.

Journal of Criminal Law and Criminology, vol. 98, no. 4, pp. 1467-1500, Summer 2008. Abstract: This article describes the constitutional problems with legally proscribing virtual age play under either child pornography or obscenity law. Second Life is a popular virtual world created by Linden Research, Incorporated. While there are many kinds of virtual environments, many of which are text-based, massively multiplayer online game (MMOG) environments are the most real-world environments, in appearance and in the way that users can interact with their surroundings and with each other. A user navigates through these virtual worlds as an avatar that a user can design to look like anything, including a child; avatars are free to do whatever their creators please including having sex. While some adults design avatars that look like monsters or celebrities, others prefer to adopt a childlike appearance. Some adults also favor less socially acceptable activities and use their young counterparts for virtual age play or sexual role play occurring in a virtual world where one avatar appears to be a child and the other an adult; this theme has become a very popular and newsworthy online pastime. This article begins with an explanation of virtual age play and an overview of the laws that bear on its legal standing, followed by a discussion of why regulation of such activity under child pornography law is inappropriate. The article concludes by exploring the potential regulation of virtual age play under obscenity law, ultimately rejecting that strategy as an unconstitutional restriction of free speech and individual liberty. This article notes that not only is there no proof that the man who is stimulated by cybersex with a virtual child is any more likely to seek our real sex with a real child but that there may be some therapeutic value in indulging such fantasies.

Pornography Use And Sexual Aggression: The Impact Of Frequency And Type Of Pornography Use On Recidivism Among Sexual Offenders.

Kingston, Drew A.; Fedoroff, Paul; Firestone, Philip; Curry, Susan; Bradford, John M.

Aggressive Behavior, Jul/Aug2008, Vol. 34, Issue 4, p341-351, 11p.

Abstract: In this study, we examined the unique contribution of pornography consumption to the longitudinal prediction of criminal recidivism in a sample of 341 child molesters. We specifically tested the hypothesis, based on predictions informed by the confluence model of sexual aggression that pornography will be a risk factor for recidivism only for those individuals classified as relatively high risk for re-offending. Pornography use (frequency and type) was assessed through self-report and recidivism was measured using data from a national database from the Royal Canadian Mounted Police. Indices of recidivism, which were assessed up to 15 years after release, included an overall criminal recidivism index, as well as subcategories focusing on violent (including sexual) recidivism and sexual recidivism alone. Results for both frequency and type of pornography use were generally consistent with our predictions. Most importantly, after controlling for general and specific risk factors for sexual aggression, pornography added significantly to the prediction of recidivism. Statistical interactions indicated that frequency of pornography use was primarily a risk factor for higher-risk offenders, when compared with lower-risk offenders, and that content of pornography (i.e., pornography containing deviant content) was a risk factor for all groups. The importance of conceptualizing particular risk factors (e.g., pornography), within the context of other individual characteristics is discussed.

The Internet and Child Sexual Offending: A Criminological Review.

Beech, Anthony R; Elliott, Ian A; Birgden, Astrid; Findlater, Donald.

Aggression and Violent Behavior, vol. 13, no. 3, pp. 2 16-228, June-July 2008.

Abstract: This paper outlines the current literature on what is known about the processes by which individuals utilize the Internet for child sexual abuse. First, three ways in which the Internet is utilized are outlined: (1) by dissemination of sexually abusive images of children for personal and/or commercial reasons; (2) by communication with other individuals with a sexual interest in children: and (3) by maintaining and developing online pedophilic networks. Second, content and availability of abusive images are described, and the difficulties faced by criminal justice agencies in both the definition of abusive images and their prohibition is discussed. Third, the potential for offenders to 'cross-over' from online offenses to contact sexual victimization of children is examined and placed within a context of various Internet offender typologies that have been developed. Finally, implications of this body of research for law and public policy are considered.

"In My Own World": A Case Study of a Paedophile's Thinking and Doing and His Use of the Internet.

Wilson, David; Jones, Timothy.

Howard Journal of Criminal Justice, vol. 47, no. 2, pp. 107 - 120, May 2008.

Abstract: This case study of a convicted pedophile ("James") in England focuses on the links between his "thinking and doing," i.e., the interaction of his fantasy life, his use of the Internet, and his contact offenses against children. For James, his thoughts, sexual desires, impulses, and fantasies were objectified and reinforced by pornographic images and videos viewed on the Internet, which were acted out in sexual contact with children. Thus, he was unrestrained in bringing his thinking, fantasizing, and visualization into the real world of sexual contact with children. The authors note that the proposed model drawn from James' case study does not suggest that every individual who has fantasies of unlawful or deviant sexual acts will inevitably act on them in the real world. For most who engage in such fantasies, they coexist with a conscience conditioned by societal norms, empathy, and histories of conditioned normative behaviors aimed at doing no harm to others in the real world of consensual intimate sexual interactions. The danger comes when individuals, like James, with deviant sexual fantasies do not have a coexisting powerful reservoir of restraints based in social and genetic conditions that keep "thinking" from becoming "doing." The case study of James derived from access granted to a convicted pedophile serving his sentence at HMP Grendon, a facility unique in the penal system of England and Wales in its operation as a therapeutic community. James was interviewed on four occasions, with each interview lasting, on average, 2 hours. All four interviews were taped, transcribed, and analyzed. 1 figure and 28 references

Online "Predators" and Their Victims: Myths, Realities, and Implications for Prevention and Treatment.

Wolak, J., Finkelhor, D., Mitchell, K., and Ybarra, M.

American Psychologist, 63(2), 111-128, 2008.

Abstract: The publicity about online “predators” who prey on naïve children using trickery and violence is largely inaccurate. Internet sex crimes involving adults and juveniles more often fit a model of statutory rape—adult offenders who meet, develop relationships with, and openly seduce underage teenagers—than a model of forcible sexual assault or pedophilic child molesting. This is a serious problem, but one that requires approaches different from those in current prevention messages emphasizing parental control and the dangers of divulging personal information. Developmentally appropriate prevention strategies that target youths directly and acknowledge normal adolescent interests in romance and sex are needed. These should provide younger adolescents with awareness and avoidance skills while educating older youths about the pitfalls of sexual relationships with adults and their criminal nature. Particular attention should be paid to higher risk youths, including those with histories of sexual abuse, sexual orientation concerns, and patterns of off- and online risk taking. Mental health practitioners need information about the dynamics of this problem and the characteristics of victims and offenders because they are likely to encounter related issues in a variety of contexts.

Sexual Fantasy In Paedophile Offenders: Can Any Model Explain Satisfactorily New Findings From A Study Of Internet And Contact Sexual Offenders?

Sheldon, Kerry; Howitt, Dennis.

Legal and Criminological Psychology, Feb2008, Vol. 13 Issue 1, p137-158, 22p.

Abstract: Purpose. Abstract: There is widespread acceptance that sexual fantasy plays a role in sexual offences but little clarity as the nature of this relationship. This paper seeks to understand better the role of fantasy in offending behaviour through the study of sexual fantasy in Internet child pornography offenders when compared with contact offenders. Differences in the patterns of sexual fantasy associated with the different offender types are explored in order to understand how fantasy content is associated with contact offences with children and desisting from such direct acting out. Methods. Participants were all convicted of child sexual offences and recruited with the help of the probation and prison services. Out of these, 16 were Internet-only offenders, 25 were contact offenders with no history of Internet offending and 10 were offenders with a mixed contact and Internet offending history. A variety of self-completion questionnaires including fantasy were completed on an individual basis together with a detailed interview. Results. The most common sexual fantasies were typical adult-male heterosexual fantasies though a variety of child-oriented and other fantasies were also common.

Contact offenders reported fewer girl-oriented sexual fantasies although the groups did not differ in terms of terms of boy-oriented fantasies. There was evidence that confrontational fantasies were commoner among contact offenders than Internet offenders. There are relationships between early sexual experiences and fantasy but peer sexual contacts seemed to be important rather than sexual abuse. Conclusion. Generally, the contact offenders seem to have less sexual fantasy pertinent to their offending than did Internet offenders. Fantasy deficit may be involved in contact offending against children

A New Playground: Sexual Predators And Pedophiles Online: Criminalizing Cyber Sex Between Adults And Minors.

Lovejoy, Tyler Patrick.

Saint Thomas Law Review. 20.2 (Winter 2008): 311-357.

Abstract: It has been exposed that within the age of the Internet, where forums and imaginative methods for achieving and performing illegal activities have been spawned, additional, and in some instances supplementary, legislation is necessary in order to protect innocent members of society from such crimes. As this comment has elucidated, those innocent persons are children, and are shown to be most susceptible to the approaches and desired fulfillment of the impulses of the sexual predator.

Characteristics of Internet Child Pornography Offenders: A Comparison with Child Molesters. L Webb, J Craissati, S Keen.

Sexual Abuse, 2007 Dec; 19(4):449-65.

Abstract: The aim of this exploratory study was to compare internet sex offenders with a matched group of child molesters in the Greater London Area. Over an 8-month period 210 subjects were assessed, of whom 90 were internet sex offenders and 120 were child molesters. A wide range of background data was collected, including a number of psychometric measures to determine risk and personality traits. The research identified a number of similarities between internet sex offenders and child molesters on background variables. Specifically, in comparison to the child molesters, the internet offenders reported more psychological difficulties in adulthood and fewer prior sexual convictions. The socio-affective characteristics of internet offenders and child molesters look similar, but the antisocial variables, such as, 'acting out' and breaking social rules underlines their difference. The follow up research was carried out after a short period of time at risk—averaging 18 months—but suggested that internet sex offenders were significantly less likely to fail in the community than child molesters in terms of all types of recidivism.

The Role Of Cognitive Distortions In Paedophilic Offending: Internet And Contact Offenders Compared.

Howitt, Dennis; Sheldon, Kerry.

Psychology, Crime and Law, Oct2007, Vol. 13 Issue 5, p469-486, 18p, 5 charts.

Abstract: Cognitive distortions are held to contribute to sexual offending against children in a number of theoretical explanations of such crimes. However, not only is there little or no direct evidence in support of the centrality of cognitive distortions in offending but recent research has questioned whether the concept has explanatory power. Cognitive distortions are variously seen as necessary for the offender to offend against children, as post-offending justifications for the offence, or as reflecting distorted patterns in the offender's upbringing. This paper explores the role of cognitive distortions in sex offending by comparing the distortions of contact sex offenders against children with Internet child pornography offenders without contact offences against children. A new cognitive distortions questionnaire was developed which was suitable for administration to Internet offenders who had no contact offences against children as well as being suitable for contact offenders. It was found that some cognitive distortions are frequently agreed with by sex offenders against children whereas others were seldom or never agreed with. Little support was found for earlier typological approaches to the cognitive schema of sex offenders against children. Contrary to the expectation that contact offenders would have more cognitive distortions, it was found that Internet offenders had more cognitive distortions that children are sexual beings. Furthermore, there were no differences in cognitive distortions justifying the offence. However, offenders with a previous history of offending were more likely to admit to cognitive distortions which justify their offending. It is accepted that cognitive distortions are readily recognized in interviews with sex offenders against children. Nevertheless, it is argued that there is a need for new research to stimulate a new understanding of the nature and role of cognitive distortions in sex offending.

Predatory Online Behavior: Modus Operandi of Convicted Sex Offenders in Identifying Potential Victims and Contacting Minors Over the Internet.

Malesky Jr., L. Alvin.

Journal of Child Sexual Abuse, 2007, Vol. 16 Issue 2, p23-32, 10p, 1 chart.

Abstract: Sex offenders have used the Internet to identify and contact minors for sexual exploitation (Armagh, 1998: Hernandez. 2000; Lamb, 1998; Lanning, 1998). Yet little is known about how these individuals select their online victims. In order to gain a better understanding of this behavior, the online activity of 31 men who perpetrated or attempted to perpetrate contact sex offenses against minors they communicated with via the Internet, was examined. Three- fourths of the participants monitored chat room dialogue and almost one-half reviewed online profiles of minors in an attempt to identify potential victims. Recommendations to increase the online safety of children and adolescents are discussed.

Current Responses to Sexual Grooming: Implication for Prevention.

Craven, Samantha; Brown, Sarah; Gilchrist, Elizabeth.

Howard Journal of Criminal Justice, vol. 46, no. 1, pp. 60-71, Feb 2007.

Abstract: This article aims to outline current responses to sexual grooming; specific attention will be given to new legislation introduced in England and Wales under the Sexual Offences Act 2003. Following an outline of this new legislation, consideration will be given to its effectiveness, including practical difficulties that are likely to restrict its scope. Issues to be discussed include: poor definition and understanding of sexual grooming, scope of legislation in relation to non-Internet grooming, difficulties in identifying sexual grooming, and a failure of the new legislation to be truly preventative. The article concludes by supporting Richard Laws's suggestion that the most effective prevention of child sexual abuse would result from adopting a public health approach. Adapted from the source document.

The Evidence Of Harm To Adults Relating To Exposure To Extreme Pornographic Material: A Rapid Evidence Assessment.

Catherine Itzin, Ann Taket and Liz Kelly.

Ministry of Justice, United Kingdom, 2007.

Abstract: This document reports on a rapid evidence assessment (REA) of the evidence of harm to adults relating to exposure to extreme pornographic materials. It was conducted for the Home Office and Department of Health as part of a programme of research being conducted by the Department of Health on the health and mental health effects of prostitution, pornography and trafficking, rape and sexual assault, and sexual offending. This REA was commissioned by the Home Office before the Ministry of Justice was formed.

Child Pornography Offenses Are a Valid Diagnostic Indicator of Pedophilia.

Seto, Michael C.; Blanchard, Ray; Cantor, James M.

Journal of Abnormal Psychology, Aug2006, Vol. 115 Issue 3, p610-615, 6p, 3 graphs.

Abstract: This study investigated whether being charged with a child pornography offense is a valid diagnostic indicator of pedophilia, as represented by an index of phallometrically assessed sexual arousal to children. The sample of 685 male patients was referred between 1995 and 2004 for a sexological assessment of their sexual interests and behavior. As a group, child pornography offenders showed greater sexual arousal to children than to adults and differed from groups of sex offenders against children, sex offenders against adults, and general sexology patients. The results suggest child pornography offending is a stronger diagnostic indicator of pedophilia than is sexually offending against child victims. Theoretical and clinical implications are discussed.

Characteristics and Behaviors of Sexual Compulsives Who Use the Internet for Sexual Purposes.

Daneback, Kristian; Ross, Michael W.; Månsson, Sven-Axel.

Sexual Addiction and Compulsivity, Jan2006, Vol. 13 Issue 1, p53-67, 15p, 2 charts.

Abstract: This study aimed to investigate the characteristics of those who engage in online sexual activities and who are sexually compulsive according to the Kalichman sexual compulsivity scale. It also aimed to investigate if online sexual activities had changed the sexually compulsive respondents' offline sexual behaviors, such as reading adult magazines, viewing adult movies, and/or having casual sex partners. Data were collected in 2002 through an online questionnaire in Swedish, which was administered via the Swedish portal *Passagen.se.* Approximately 6% of the 1458 respondents who answered the 10-item sexual compulsivity scale were defined as sexually compulsive. A multivariate regression analysis showed sexually compulsives more likely to be men, to live in a relationship, to be bisexual, and to have had an STI. The time spent online for sexual purposes was found to be a measure of the kind of sexual activity rather than a measure of online sexual compulsivity. A bivariate analysis of nominal data showed that engagement in online sexual activities made respondents quit, decrease, maintain or increase their offline sexual behaviors. Sexual compulsive respondents were found to increase their offline pornography consumption to a greater extent than did non-sexually compulsives.

Paedophilia On The Internet--A Study Of 33 Convicted Offenders In The Canton Of Lucerne. Frei A, Erenay N, Dittmann V, Graf M.

Swiss Medical Weekly, 2005 Aug 20; Vol. 135 (33-34), pp. 488-94.

Abstract: Background: The connection between the consumption of pornography and "contact crimes" is unclear. The Internet has facilitated the mass consumption of pornography in general and specifically illegal pornography such as child pornography. In 1999, the owners of "Landslide Production Inc.", an international provider of child-pornography in the USA were arrested and the credit-card-numbers of their clients were put at the disposal of the law enforcement agencies of the countries concerned.

Methods: Roughly 1300 Swiss citizens were subsequently arrested in the course of the nationwide action "Genesis". In the canton of Lucerne 33 men were identified. The police-files of these men were screened for psychosocial, criminological and psychosexual data. Results:

Most of these middle-aged men held comparatively elevated professional positions, only ten were married, eleven had never had an intimate relationship to a woman, and only thirteen of them had children. Only one of them had a relevant criminal record. The level of abuse depicted in the illegal material was high, all but one consumed pornography from other fields of sexual deviation. The personal statements of the offenders in general were hardly reliable, in three cases, however, the diagnosis of sexual deviation could be established from the files. The estimated time some of the offenders must have spent online in order to retrieve the material allows the diagnosis of Pathological Internet-Use. Conclusions: Deviant sexual fantasies seem to be widespread also among men otherwise not registered for any offences. The consumption of even particularly disgusting material may not be a specific risk factor for "contact" crimes.

Internet Offenders: Traders, Travelers, and Combination Trader-Travelers.

Alexy, Eileen M.; Burgess, Ann W.; Baker, Timothy.

Journal of Interpersonal Violence, vol. 20, no. 7, pp. 804-8 12, July 2005.

Abstract: The Internet opens a vast array of communication, entertainment, and educational resources for children; however, it also opens a gateway to home and school for offenders who wish to exploit children. A convenience sample of 225 cases published in the news media was examined. The cases were classified using law enforcement terminology to describe

Internet offenders as traders, travelers, or combination trader-travelers. The media is seen as a critical source of information for the public to be aware of how the Internet is being used to commit sexual exploitation and sex crimes against children.

The Criminal Histories And Later Offending Of Child Pornography Offenders.

Seto MC, Eke AW.

Sexual Abuse: A Journal of Research and Treatment, 2005 Apr; Vol. 17 (2), pp. 201-10.

Abstract: The likelihood that child pornography offenders will later commit a contact sexual offense is unknown. In the present study, we identified a sample of 201 adult male child pornography offenders using police databases and examined their charges or convictions after the index child pornography offense(s). We also examined their criminal records to identify potential predictors of later offenses: 56% of the sample had a prior criminal record, 24% had prior contact sexual offenses, and 15% had prior child pornography offenses. One-third were concurrently charged with other crimes at the time they were charged for child pornography offenses. The average time at risk was 2.5 years; 17% of the sample offended again in some way during this time, and 4% committed a new contact sexual offense. Child pornography offenders with prior criminal records were significantly more likely to offend again in any way during the follow-up period. Child pornography offenders who had committed a prior or concurrent contact sexual offense were the most likely to offend again, either generally or sexually.

From Fantasy to Reality: The Link Between Viewing Child Pornography and Molesting Children.

Kim, Candice.

Prosecutor, vol. 39, no. 2, pp. 17-18, 20, - 47, March/April 2005.

Abstract: This article argues that viewing child pornography is linked to child molestation. Some individuals claim that viewing child pornography is just viewing pictures and does not actually harm children. On the contrary, the author argues that images of child pornography are evidence of past, present, and future child sexual abuse. According to statistics generated by the United States Postal Inspection Service, 80 percent of child pornography purchasers are active abusers and almost 40 percent of the child pornographers investigated during the past several years have sexually molested children in the past. Moreover, a study completed in 2000 by the Director of the Sex Offender Treatment Program at the Butner Federal Correctional Complex in North Carolina revealed that of 54 inmates convicted of child pornography offenses, 79.6% of them admitted that they had also molested significant numbers of children. Child sexual abusers frequently use pornographic images to groom child victims prior to committing sexual abuse. Repeated exposure to pornographic images involving children serves to normalize child sexual abuse and desensitize the child to such behaviors. Evidence gathered from law enforcement investigations has indicated that offenders who have collections of child pornography are often also actively engaged in child sexual abuse with the children depicted in the pictures. As such, it is clear that owning and viewing child pornographic pictures extends beyond merely looking at pictures and most often involves the actual sexual abuse of children in the past, present, and future of the offender. Therefore, perpetrators who possess child pornography should be vigilantly pursued by law enforcement as likely child sexual abusers.

The Internet and Family and Acquaintance Sexual Abuse.
Mitchell, Kimberly J.; Finkelhor, David; Wolak, Janis.
Child Maltreatment, vol. 10, no. 1, pp. 49-60, Feb 2005.

Abstract: This article explores the dynamics of cases involving family and acquaintance sexual offenders who used the Internet to commit sex crimes against minors. Although the stereotype of Internet crimes involves unknown adults meeting juvenile victims online, Internet use can also play a role in sexual crimes against minors by family members and acquaintances. Data were collected from a national sample of law enforcement agencies about arrests for Internet-related sex crimes against minors. Family and acquaintance offenders were nearly as numerous as offenders who used the Internet to meet victims online. They used the Internet in various ways to further their crimes including as a tool to seduce or groom, store or disseminate sexual images of victims, arrange meetings and communicate, reward victims, or advertise or sell victims. Prevention messages and investigation approaches should be revised to incorporate awareness of such cases and their dynamics.

Commercial And Sexual Exploitation Of of Children And Young People(CSEC) in the UK—A Review.
Chase, Elaine; Statham, June.
Child Abuse Review, Jan/Feb2005, Vol. 14 Issue 1, p4-25, 22p.

Abstract: This paper reviews recent information and data relevant to the commercial sexual exploitation of children and young people in the UK. Three main aspects of exploitation are addressed: abuse through prostitution; abuse through pornography; and the trafficking of children and young people to and through the UK for the purposes of commercial sexual exploitation. Most published research in this area relates to young people exploited through prostitution. The review explores the range of vulnerability factors, the processes used to engage young people in prostitution and the types of support strategies for those being exploited. Rather less information is currently available on the scale of child pornography, or the links between the use of pornography and other forms of sexual abuse. The internet as a modern technology for proliferating child pornography is discussed, alongside its role in providing opportunities for paedophiles to access and 'groom' children for sexual purposes. Finally, the review provides a summary of research on trafficking of children to and through the UK for the purposes of commercial sexual exploitation and demonstrates the limited knowledge about this topic.

The Varieties of Child Pornography Production.

Wolak, J., Finkelhor, D., and Mitchell, K.J.

In Quayle, E. and Taylor, M. (Eds.), Viewing Child Pornography on the Internet: Understanding the Offense, Managing the Offender, Helping the Victims (pgs. 31-48). Dorset, UK: Russell House Publishing, 2005. URL: http://www.unh.edu/ccrc/pdf/jvq/CV100.pdf

Abstract: Examines a sample of U.S. criminal cases in which offenders arrested for Internet- related crimes against minors took pictures of victims.

Child Pornography Possessors Arrested in Internet-Related Crimes: Findings from the National Juvenile Online Victimization Study.

Wolak, J., Finkelhor, D., and Mitchell, K.J.

National Center for Missing & Exploited Children, Alexandria: VA, 2005.

URL: http://www.unh.edu/ccrc/pdf/jvq/CV81.pdf

Abstract: The goals of the National Juvenile Online Victimization (N-JOV) Study were to survey law-enforcement agencies within the United States (U.S.) to count arrests for Internet-related sex crimes committed against minors and describe the characteristics of the offenders, the crimes they committed, and their victims. This report focuses on a representative national sample of arrested offenders who possessed child pornography.

Use of Pornography during the Commission of Sexual Offenses.

Langevin, Ron; Curnoe, Suzanne.

International Journal of Offender Therapy and Comparative Criminology, vol. 48, no. 5, pp. 572 - 586, October 2004.

Abstract: This study investigated any links between sex offenders' use of pornography (materials that are sexually arousing) and their sex offenses. An overview of the literature on this topic focuses on sex offenders' use of pornography for self-stimulation, to groom the victims, and for later self-gratification and monetary gain. The current study involved a sample of 124 cases (Sample 1) from the authors' private practice; in every case, the offenders were asked about their use of pornography and its role in their sex offenses. Police reports were also available in the majority of cases and were used in interviews with the offenders. In order to examine whether trends in the use of pornography by sex offenders has changed over the past 30 years, a historical sample of 437 cases was drawn from a database of 2,125 sex-offender cases collected from 1970 to 1991 at the Clarke Institute of Psychiatry (Sample 2). Of the 561 cases studied, only 17 percent involved the use of pornography immediately prior to or during the offense. These findings suggest that the mere possession of pornography does not in itself lead to the commission of a sexual crime. Although 47 percent of the offenders had pornography in their possession prior to their crimes, only 17 percent used it for self-stimulation either immediately prior to the crime or during the crime. Offenders against children used pornography more than offenders against adults (42 percent compared with 19 percent). There was no indication of a change in patterns of pornography over time in Sample 2; however, the increased availability of pornography through the Internet may change this pattern in the foreseeable future.

Getting to Grips with Sexual Grooming? The New Offence under the Sexual Offences Act 2003. Ost, Suzanne.

The Journal of Social Welfare and Family Law, vol. 26, no. 2, pp.147-159, 2004.

Abstract: In recent years, there has been increased societal concern regarding the dangers posed to children by sexual abuse and other related acts. For the main part, this article examines the new UK offense of meeting a child following sexual grooming under Section 15 of the Sexual Offences Act 2003. I will address the question of whether the introduction of this offense is likely to meet the government's aim of providing greater protection for children against behavior associated with sexual abuse. In particular, I will consider how difficult it will be to prove the existence of a harmful ulterior intent in order to make out the offense and why the government has opted to create this specific offense rather than utilize the existing law of criminal attempt. I will argue that the new offense is a step in the right direction and that the current protection offered to children will be significantly extended by its introduction. 17 References. Adapted from the source document.

Pedophilia and Sexual Offenses Against Children.
Seto, Michael C.
Annual Review of Sex Research, 2004, Vol. 15, p329-369, 41p.
Abstract: Investigates pedophilia and sexual offenses against children. Role of neurodevelopmental problems and childhood sexual abuse in the etiology of pedophilia; Self- identification pedophiles; Methods for assessing pedophilia; Possession of child pornography as a behavioral indicator of pedophilic interests.

Model of Problematic Internet Use in People with a Sexual Interest in Children.
Ethel Quayle, Max Taylor.
CyberPsychology and Behavior. January 2003, 6(1): 93-106.
Abstract: Agencies working with sex offenders are starting to see the emergence of people with a sexual interest in children who meet some of their needs through the use of child pornography, or the seduction of children, through the Internet. While CBT models dominate our understanding of sex offenders, there has been little research into the role that such new technologies may play in offending behavior. Data from the COPINE project has been used to generate a model of such offending behavior that emphasizes the role of cognitions in both the etiology, engagement with and problematic use of the Internet for those with a sexual interest in children. Such a model seeks to incorporate contemporary thinking about the role of cognitions in Pathological Internet Use, but applies this from a nonpathological perspective. This model is a first step towards providing a conceptual framework for such offending that will help inform both assessment and therapy.

Pedophilia on the Internet.
Deirmenjian, John M.
Journal of Forensic Sciences, vol. 47, no. 5, pp. 1090 - 1092, September 2002.
Abstract: In analyzing cases of pedophiles' use of the Internet to exploit child victims, this paper discusses two models of pedophilia: a trust-based

seductive model and a direct sexual model; it also explores the role that mental health professionals can play in the assessment of pedophilia manifested through the Internet. Under the trust-based seductive model of pedophilia manifested on the Internet, a pedophile seeks to gain the attention of a targeted child user of the Internet. The pedophile's goal is to obtain a child's trust through an escalation of attention intended to result in the seduction of a child into sexual acts through a face-to-face meeting. The predator can claim to be of the same sex as an intended victim in order to gain the potential victim's trust. Similarly, by pretending to be in the same age group, an unsuspecting child will consider the pedophile a peer. As conversations develop, a pedophile informs the child that he shares similar interests and common experiences. This paper summarizes four cases in which such a model of seduction was used on the Internet. Under the direct sexual model, a pedophile uses Internet communications in taking a relatively short time to introduce the subject of sex with a potential victim. There may be a trade of images of child or adult pornography. Pedophiles use Internet bulletin boards to trade child pornography or to obtain lists of children who have had a prior association with pedophiles. As in the trust-based model, the ultimate goal is usually to arrange a meeting in person. Two cases of this type of use of the Internet are presented. If parents observe disturbing changes in their child's behavior, they may seek the assistance of a child psychologist or psychiatrist.: A mental health professional who is sufficiently informed about the Internet exploitation of children may detect victimization from subtle clues. Also, an awareness of the phenomenon of "cyberstalking" and pedophilia on the Internet can facilitate a thorough evaluation of a pedophile in a forensic setting. Further, government intervention can help prevent child sexual exploitation through the Internet. The Federal Trade Commission is currently seeking legislation that requires Internet companies to get parental consent before permitting children under the age of 13 to enter Internet sites that solicit addresses, phone numbers, and personal information. In addition, the FBI is involved in training State and local law enforcement officials in how to establish cyber police units to patrol the Internet. The National Center for Missing & Exploited Children has established a "cyber-tipline" for the public to use in reporting any suspicious or illicit activity that involves children on the Internet. 12 references.

Child Pornography And The Internet: Perpetuating A Cycle Of Abuse.
Quayle, Ethel; Taylor, Max.
Deviant Behavior, Jul2002, Vol. 23 Issue 4, p33 1-361, 31p.

Abstract: Thirteen men convicted of downloading child pornography were interviewed with a view to understanding how these men talked about the photographs and the function such talk played in their accounts. The interviews were informed by earlier work with defended subjects and were analyzed within a discursive framework. Quotations are used from the interviews to illustrate the analysis. Six principal discourses emerged within these accounts in relation to child pornography: sexual arousal; as collectibles; facilitating social relationships; as a way of avoiding real life; as therapy; and in relation to the Internet. These are discussed in the context of previous research. The analysis illustrates the important role that the Internet plays in increasing sexual arousal to child pornography and highlights individual differences in whether this serves as a substitute or as a blueprint for contact offenses. It also draws our attention to the important role that community plays in the Internet and how collecting facilitates the objectification of children and increases the likelihood that in the quest for new images children continue to be sexually abused. Discourses focusing on both therapy and addiction serve to distance the respondent from personal agency and allow for continued engagement with child pornography.

Child Seduction and Self-Representation on the Internet.

Quayle, Ethel; Taylor, Max.

CyberPsychology and Behavior, Oct2001, Vol. 4 Issue 5, p597-608, 12p.

Abstract: This paper presents a case study of a man charged with the offense of downloading child pornography from the Internet. He had used the Internet to traffic child pornography, and, in addition, to locate children to abuse, to engage in inappropriate sexual communication with children, and to communicate with other pedophiles. Such offenses were facilitated by self-representing in Chat rooms as both a child and an adult. The case study illustrates how such offenders move through a repertoire of offending behavior and discusses the role that the Internet can play in supporting inappropriate and disinhibited sexual behavior that victimizes children through the trading of child pornography and possible child seduction. The Internet is seen to play a unique role in allowing individuals to self-represent aspects that might otherwise remain hidden or dormant.

The Internet and Offending Behaviour: A Case Study.

Quayle, E.; Linehan, C.; Holland, G.; Taylor, M.

The Journal of Sexual Aggression, 2000, Vol. 6 Issue 1/2, p78-96, 19p.

Abstract: The COPINE Project at the Department of Applied Psychology, seeks to address children's vulnerability in relation to the Internet and child pornography. As part of the project, offenders convicted of downloading such images have been interviewed. This paper considers existing models of offender behaviour alongside literature relating to Internet use. A single case study is used to illustrate a process-focused model of offending, using interview material to demonstrate how the offender represented and accounted for his behaviour. The offender in question had no history of engaging in sexual behaviour with actual children, but his case illustrated many of the stages described by offenders in their involvement with pornography, including: setting events, engagement, collecting behaviour, and the emergence of relationships.

Cybersex Users, Abuse, and Compulsives: New Findings and Implications.

Cooper, A.; Delmonico, D.L.; Buro, R.

Sexual Addiction and Compulsivity; January 2000 Vol. 7, p5-29, 25p.

Abstract: Literature regarding sexual use of the Internet has primarily focused on anecdotal data of clinical cases. This study empirically examines the characteristics and usage patterns of individuals who use the Internet for sexual purposes. The Kalichman Sexual Compulsivity Scale was the primary tool used to divide the sample (n = 9,265) into four groups: nonsexually compulsive (n = 7,738), moderately sexually compulsive (n = 1,007), sexually compulsive (n = 424), and cybersex compulsive (n = 96); 17% of the entire sample scored in the problematic range for sexual compulsivity. Data analysis of the four groups indicated statistically significant differences on descriptive characteristics such as gender, sexual orientation, relationship status, and occupation. In addition, patterns of use differed across groups including the primary method of pursuing sexual materials, primary location of accessing sexual material, and the extent to which cybersex has interfered with a respondent's life. This study is one of the few quantitative examinations of the patterns of problematic and compulsive use of the Internet for sexual purposes. Implications and suggestions for research, public education, and professional trainings are presented.

Revisiting the Use of Pornography by Sexual Offenders: Implications for Theory and Practice.

W. L. Marshall.

Journal of Sexual Aggression, Volume 6, Issue 1 and 2 January 2000, pages 67 – 77. Abstract: This article examines the extant research on the use of pornography by sexual offenders and some of the debates engendered by such use. The analyses should assist in clarifying a number of issues of concern for all who work in the field of sexual offending.

Relationship between Child Pornography and the Commission of Sexual Offences against Children: A Review of the Literature.

Rettinger, L Jill.

Canada Dept of Justice, 2000.

URL: http://canada.justice.gc.ca/eng/pi/rs/rep-rap/2000/rr00_5.pdf

Abstract: This paper describes the current state of knowledge of the role pornography plays in sexual offenses against children. Two main research questions are addressed: (1) to what extent do pedophiles consume pornography, particularly child pornography, and (2) how is pornography used by pedophiles? A review of clinical and retrospective studies from the social science literature, as well as published anecdotal reports and expert opinions, is undertaken in order to probe the link between adult and child pornography and child sexual abuse. The literature review revealed very little empirical research on the topic, making it difficult to draw conclusions. Research concerning the use of child pornography by pedophiles has been mostly anecdotal, and the few empirical studies on the topic have been plagued by inconsistencies in definitions and problems involving sampling methods and procedures. Although anecdotal evidence suggests that some pedophiles use child pornography, there is no indication of the proportion of child molesters who use this type of material. Retrospective studies of pornography use by sex offenders suggest that a large percentage of sex offenders do use adult pornography, but comparative studies have failed to find a difference in the pornography consumption rates of sex offenders versus non-sex offenders, especially concerning the use of soft-core materials. The author recommends further research on the use of hard-core pornography before conclusions are drawn. Furthermore retrospective clinical studies have found that most sex offenders, including child sexual offenders, report minimal or no exposure to child pornography, which is a departure from the findings of anecdotal reports. However, these differences may be a function of discrepancies in the definition of child pornography. Seven main motivations were found in the literature for how pedophiles use child pornography; they include the motivations of justification, arousal, profit, preservation of victim s youth, lower victim s inhibition, blackmail, and medium of exchange. Most anecdotal reports on the use of pornography describe the use of these materials to disinhibit victims of abuse and as items of trade with other pedophiles. In conclusion, a direct causal link between pornography and child sexual abuse is not supported by the current state of knowledge.

Annotated Bibliography: Child Exploitation

The Never-Ending Limits of § 230: Extending ISP Immunity to the Sexual Exploitation of Children.

Noeth, Katy.

Federal Communications Law Journal, May2009, Vol. 61 Issue 3, p765-784, 20p.

Abstract: In 2006, the U.S. District Court for the Eastern District of Texas extended civil liability to Yahoo! under § 230 of the Communications Decency Act so that it could not be sued for knowingly profiting from a Web site where members exchanged sexually explicit pictures of minors. The court found that the reasoning of the seminal § 230 case, Zeran v. AOL, was analogous and that policy considerations mandated its holding. This Note argues that a multifaceted approach is needed to prevent future courts from following that decision, including an amendment to § 230 that would impose civil liability upon ISPs that knowingly allow the sexual exploitation of children on their Web sites. In the meantime, however, future courts should distinguish Zeran and refuse to apply its defamation rationale to child sexual exploitation claims. Future courts should also refuse to extend the Immunity to child sexual exploitation claims because doing so does not further the congressional intent behind § 230. Courts should recognize an exception to immunity under § 230(e)(1) in order to protect minors on the Internet.

Identifying and Managing Stress in Child Pornography and Child Exploitation Investigators. Krause, Meredith.

Journal of Police and Criminal Psychology, vol. 24, no. 1, pp. 22-29, Apr 2009.

Abstract: In the last decade, law enforcement personnel have increasingly been tasked to police the internet in an effort to staunch the production and distribution of child pornography and to investigate computer-facilitated child exploitation. These investigative personnel have encountered a range of assignment-specific challenges and strains as a result of their involvement in this taxing and novel investigative activity. In some cases, the cumulative effects of these strains, together with repeated exposure to highly disturbing images of abused children, have resulted in stress reactions that have commanded the attention of police managers and police psychologists alike. The present article is intended to provide an overview of the stresses unique to child exploitation and pornography investigations, common reactions to these stressors, procedural safeguards to mitigate the impact of this high-risk assignment, and two model programs designed to meet the needs of the current generation of 'cyber cops'.

Preventing Sexual Abuse of Children in the Twenty-First Century: Preparing for Challenges and Opportunities.

Wurtele, Sandy K.

Journal of Child Sexual Abuse, vol. 18, no. 1, pp. 1 - 18, January-February 2009.

Abstract: This paper describes the scope and consequences of child sexual abuse (CSA) and critiques child-focused personal safety educational programs designed to prevent sexual victimization. CSA is an extremely complex social problem that will require comprehensive solutions to eradicate. Prevention of CSA is best conceptualized as a process of reducing risk factors and building protective factors in the potential perpetrator, potential victim and his or her family, and in the environment in which they all exist. Major health and social problems will be eradicated only when all sectors of society, not just the individual, share responsibility for solutions. An effective prevention program for youth emphasized the need to target an array of settings, including schools, homes, and communities. Consistent with these ecological models, four populations that need to be targeted for a comprehensive approach to CSA prevention are: children/youth, parents, professionals, and the public. For each target, suggestions for primary prevention efforts are offered, and opportunities and challenges are described. Although tertiary prevention efforts, such as treating offenders and victims, are crucial for eradicating the problem, one section describes population-focused interventions that occur with essentially well people with the aim of reducing the number of new incidences in the population. Results suggest that currently not enough is being done to prevent the sexual exploitation of children.

Changing Contexts of Deference to Elders, Children's Rights and Sexual Exploitation of Children in Tanzania

Bali, Theodora Axweso Luxuma.

Dissertation Abstracts International, A: The Humanities and Social Sciences, vol. 69, no. 10, pp. 4013, 2009.

Abstract: Regardless of the centrality of political and economic resources in the constructions of power, this research argues that the notions of power are contested. Exploration of the relationship between deference to elders and the vulnerability to childhood sexual exploitation with 105 young women has shown that certain actions like sexual intercourse may transmit symbolic power. Ironically, the growing poverty and increasing inaccessibility to income earning opportunities that affect Tanzanian men and women equally also provide alternative routes for women to create their new roles. Unlike in traditional communities where elders monopolized hegemonic power due to their control of ancestral rituals and clan resources, today women can turn to formal education, technology and the media for examples of alternative survival routes including unconventional ones like survival sex. This research employed informal and structured interviews to test the hypothesis that continued deference to elders within the changing context of increased urbanization, nuclear family system and paid childrearing, increases children's vulnerability to sexual exploitation. Elder interaction, understanding of child sexual exploitation, access to support network, perception of self-esteem, importance of filial respect, rural/urban background, education levels and family types, were among the examined childhood experiences. The data were analyzed for emergent themes of understanding and prevalence of child sexual exploitation, power and control, and sexual exploitation vulnerability. The results supported the hypothesis by showing that conditions of deprivation increase children's vulnerable to sexual exploitation and the model explains 39.6% of the shared variance. The contribution of this research is twofold: taking the primary step to explore the role of childrearing contexts in predicting vulnerability to sexual exploitation and ascertaining that Tanzanian children are vulnerable to sexual predation regardless of where they grow up. This is because the cultural practices that subordinate women and children have remained strong in both rural and urban areas. This dissertation is presented in seven chapters: introduction, review of relevant literature, social and cultural background of Tanzania, methods and goals, analysis and results, discussion, and conclusion.

"Little Italian Slaves": Lessons Learned from the Padrone Boys.

Jalongo, Mary.

Early Childhood Education Journal, Dec2008, Vol. 36 Issue 3, p209-212, 4p.

Abstract The author discusses teaching about the padrone system, a form of child exploitation practiced in the U.S. In the padrone system, sponsors offered to educate European children in America but employed them as indentured servants. The author notes the difficulties faced by immigrant children in schools and how human trafficking operations employ people of the same nationality as those being exploited. She suggests studying exploitation of children can illustrate progress in child welfare.

Human Trafficking: Sketchy Data and Policy Responses.
Goodey, Jo.
Criminology and Criminal Justice, vol. 8, no. 4, pp. 421 - 442, November 2008.

Abstract: This article examines trafficking in human beings and provides an overview of legislative and policy responses to the trafficking phenomenon. With increase recognition of the problem of inadequate data on trafficking, there appears to be a renewed focus on the need for better data on which to build policy responses. The developments reflect a general trend at the level of governments and international inter-governmental organizations (IGOs) to collect more robust data for policy developments, particularly in the area of crime and criminal justice. The focus of trafficking has been, since the late 1980s, predominantly on sex trafficking, with less attention paid to other areas that are equally significant in terms of magnitude and impact, though the data cannot prove this assertion one way or another. Trafficking appears to be witnessing a subtle shift with respect to its focus of attention; trafficking for labor exploitation and child trafficking are increasingly receiving more attention. While many non-governmental organizations (NGOs) and academic commentators would dispute the idea that trafficking is being responded to as a victim-centered crime, this article suggests that a shift can be noted in this direction, at the same time as trafficking continues to be responded to as part of the migration-crime-security nexus. Further, although researchers, the international community, and NGOs have recorded data on victims who experience trafficking, there is a paucity of data concerning traffickers. The other area that remains under-researched is information on the demand side of trafficking.

Confronting Sex Trafficking: Lessons From History.
Cree, Viviene E.
International Social Work, vol. 51, no. 6, pp. 763-776, Nov. 2008.

Abstract: English Sex trafficking, the trafficking of women and children for the purposes of sexual exploitation, is recognized today as a worldwide problem, affecting hundreds of thousands each year. It is not, however, a new phenomenon. This paper will discuss the lessons raised by the National Vigilance Association's response to this problem.

The Sexual Exploitation of Children and Young People in Northern Ireland: Overview from the Barnardo's Beyond the Shadows Service.

Montgomery-Devlin, Jacqui.

Child Care in Practice, Oct2008, Vol. 14 Issue 4, p381-400, 20p, 2 diagrams, 1 color. Abstract: The present paper provides an overview of child sexual exploitation in Northern Ireland and related issues. It focuses on Barnardo's response to the problem of sexual exploitation and sets it in both a historical and a contemporary context. The paper considers the importance of recognising exploitation as child abuse and addresses specific myths associated with this. It makes use of recent research and campaigning by Barnardo's to challenge and change public perception. The paper presents a range of risk factors and indicators that are used to identify children and young people who are most likely to experience or be at risk from sexual exploitation. It examines the who, what and why of sexual exploitation of children in Northern Ireland, presenting local research and anecdotal evidence to demonstrate the extent and range of the problem, while acknowledging the often hidden nature of this activity. As well as focusing on young people abused through prostitution, the paper also makes reference to the issue of human trafficking and the increasing problems of abuse via the Internet and mobile phone technology. The paper draws on international human rights standards and domestic legislation in relation to child sexual exploitation and explores the existing legislative context in Northern Ireland. Included is a summary of the Barnardo's Beyond the Shadows Service established to respond to this issue. The paper lays out the four main aims of the service and provides an overview of its work. It concludes by challenging the audience, legislators, policy-makers and service providers to respond strategically and operationally to the experiences and needs of children and young people who are sexually exploited or at risk of this.

Trafficking of Children in Albania: Patterns of Recruitment and Reintegration.

Gjermeni, Eglantina; Van Hook, Mary P; Gjipali, Saemira; Xhillari, Lindita; Lungu, Fatjon; Hazizi, Anila.

Child Abuse and Neglect, vol. 32, no. 10, pp. 941 - 948, October 2008.

Abstract: This study identifies the issues and patterns of child trafficking involving Albanian children. Findings identify the role of family poverty especially as set within a context of societal poverty and membership in a marginalized group (Gypsy), in increasing the risk of children being trafficked. Severe family dysfunction combined with ignorance of the reality of trafficking further increased the risk of being trafficked. Albanian children experienced extremely harsh conditions during trafficking. The reintegration process was difficult because of stigma, lack of community resources, ongoing family problems, and their own trauma. Social policies that do not protect victims and allow traffickers to operate without fear of punishment further support trafficking. Results identified community and family poverty, family dysfunction, ignorance regarding trafficking, inadequate legal policies and implementation, and membership in a disadvantaged group as key factors placing children at risk for the harsh world of trafficking. Prevention and protection require domestic and international partnerships to provide legal protection and the resources to address poverty, inform parents, and ameliorate family problems. Reintegration requires treatment for trauma as well as alternative educational and vocational opportunities. Data were collected from 61 children who had escaped from trafficking, 22 children from similar at-risk groups who had not been trafficked, 15 parents of currently or previously trafficked children, 10 parents had not been trafficked, 15 parents of currently or previously trafficked children, 10 parents from a similar groups whose children had not been trafficked, and 8 key informants. Table, references

Cyber Child Sexual Exploitation.

Burgess AW; Mahoney M; Visk J; Morgenbesser L.

Journal of Psychosocial Nursing and Mental Health Services, 2008 Sep; 46 (9): 38-45.

Abstract: A 2-year review of 285 child cyber crime cases reported in the newspaper revealed how the Internet offenders were apprehended, the content of child pornography, and crime classification. A subsample of 100 cases with data on offender occupation revealed 73% of cases involved people in positions of authority. The dynamics of child cyber crime cases direct the implications for nursing practice in terms of evidence-based suspicion for reporting, categorizing the content of Internet images, referral of children for counseling, and treatment of offenders.

Adolescents Accessing Indecent Images of Children.

Gillespie, Alisdair A.

Journal of Sexual Aggression, Jul2008, Vol. 14 Issue 2, p111-122, 12p.

Abstract: This paper considers the legal consequences of adolescents accessing indecent images of children. It challenges the current default position that such behaviour is illegal and worthy of punishment. The paper seeks to understand the circumstances in which adolescents may seek age-appropriate material and considers whether this is more blameworthy than those who engage in physical sexual contact with other adolescents. By examining the legal frameworks of indecent images and contact offending the paper concludes that there is unfair disparity within the criminal justice system.

The Emotional Impact on and Coping Strategies Employed by Police Teams Investigating Internet Child Exploitation.

Burns, Carolyn M; Morley, Jeff; Bradshaw, Richard; Domene, José.

Traumatology, vol. 14, no. 2, pp. 20-3 1, June 2008.

Abstract: Work on Internet child exploitation (ICE) teams require individuals to perform a number of investigative tasks, including viewing graphic images and videos of young children being sexually assaulted and tortured, to identify victims and locate perpetrators. Individuals involved in this work may be at higher risk for experiencing secondary traumatic stress because of the graphic images and sounds to which they are exposed. The impact of ICE investigations and what helps and hinders coping with the work was explored using the Critical Incident Technique with 14 members of a Royal Canadian Mounted Police integrated ICE team. Results suggest that there are a number of organizational and personal strategies that can assist those who work in this field to cope more effectively.

What Human Rights Law Obscures: Global Sex Trafficking And The Demand For Children. Dillon, Sara.

UCLA Women's Law Journal, Winter2008, Vol. 17 Issue 1, p121-186, 66p.

Abstract: The article focuses on human rights law and its implication to child sex trafficking. The demand for children to be used in a global sex industry has increased, which triggered concern among the international community. The commercial sexual exploitation of children is recognized as one of the most heinous forms of human rights violations and abuses. Moreover, the nature of the demand for trafficked children is also discussed.

Cybering, Online Grooming And Ageplay.

Kierkegaard, Sylvia.

Computer Law and Security Report, Jan2008, Vol. 24 Issue 1, p41-55, 15p.

Abstract: Abstract: Recent advances in computer technology have been aiding sexual predators, stalkers, child pornographers, child traffickers, and others with the intent of exploiting children. Internet bulletin boards, chat rooms, private websites, and peer-to-peer networks are being used daily by paedophiles to meet unsuspecting children. Compounding the problem is the lack of direct governance by an international body, which will curb the illegal content and activity. Most countries already have laws protecting children, but what is needed is a concerted law enforcement and international legislation to combat child sex abuse. With the enactment of the Convention on the Protection of Children against Sexual Exploitation and Sexual Abuse, this may soon become a reality in Europe. This current article will discuss some of the recent legal developments concerning online child protection, including the new Convention.

Victims No Longer: Research on Child Survivors of Trafficking for Sexual and Labor Exploitation in the United States, Final Report.

Gozdziak, Elzbieta; Bump, Micah N.

National Institute of Justice, 2008.

URL: http://www.ncjrs.gov/pdffiles1/nij/grants/221891.pdf

Abstract: In an attempt to improve the understanding of child trafficking and enhance the system of care, this federally supported study examined the patterns of abuse of child victims of trafficking for sexual and labor exploitation, analyzed the challenges service providers face in assisting child victims, and assessed prospects for integration of child survivors into the wider society. Several emerging themes within the realm of solutions and resolutions are identified; however, the ultimate solution is related to prevention and eradication of child trafficking. Recommendations presented in working toward solutions and resolutions include: (1) the need to earmark development resources to establish high quality educational programs in order to reduce child labor and prevent child trafficking; (2) the need for continued monitoring and assessments of both national and international initiatives to reduce child labor; (3) the need to shift away from monitoring industries and workplaces employing children to the monitoring of children removed from work; and (4) the need to enhance collaboration between actors in source and destination countries interested in reducing child labor and preventing child trafficking.

Human trafficking for sexual exploitation and forced labor is one of the fastest growing areas of criminal activity. Supported by a grant from the U.S. Department of Justice, National Institute of Justice (NIJ), this report is based on findings from a 12-month study undertaken by the Institute for the Study of International Migration (ISIM) and the Migration and Refugee Services (MRS) to examine patterns of abuse of child victims of trafficking, explore the challenges faced by service providers assisting child victims, and examine ways to integrate child survivors of trafficking into society. The research focuses on the cohort of child victims receiving services through foster care and unaccompanied refugee minors (URM) programs. By analyzing patterns of victimization before emancipation as well as post-emancipation experiences of child survivors within the United States Federal system of care, this research project attempts to expand the knowledge base of the special service needs of child victims of trafficking, enhance treatment modalities, provide an understanding of repeat victimization, and take steps to prevent it in the future.

Does the World of International Aid Need a Watchdog?

Naik, Asmita.

Forced Migration Review, no. 29, pp. 62-63, Dec 2007.

Abstract: Five years on from the scandal of sexual exploitation of West African refugee children by humanitarians, has enough been done to ensure that the system of international humanitarian assistance really does the good it is intended for? Adapted from the source document.

Interpreting the Intentions of Internet Predators: An Examination of Online Predatory Behavior. Marcum, Catherine D.

Journal of Child Sexual Abuse, vol. 16, no. 4, pp. 99 - 114, 2007.

Abstract: This study examined three chat room transcripts between adult predators and adult volunteers of the group Perverted Justice who posed as children on the internet in order to provide insight on child sexual abuse on the internet. The findings of the study indicated that of the three men whose transcripts were analyzed, all used manipulation to lure their victims; the predators bluntly indicated their sexual intentions to the adolescent females. Only one man vocalized any sort of reservation about his wrongdoing while aggressively attempting to arrange a sexual encounter. The purpose of the study was to provide an understanding of the speed and aggressive nature of online solicitation of minors for sex. Few studies have actually taken place regarding behaviors and characteristics of Internet predators.

The study had several limitations that could be improved in later research. It would be beneficial to review the communications between not only female adolescents and male adults, but also combinations of different genders of adolescents and adults as the type of conversations and deceptions techniques may be quite different between two males than between two females. A greater number of case studies should be examined to allow for a better representation of the population of Internet predators. Analysis of the lifestyles and past experiences of these predators would allow for a better understanding of their choices and activities. Perverted Justice (PeeJ) is a civilian watch group that is dedicated to exposing adult predators searching for children in chat rooms. Volunteers for PeeJ enter chat rooms and pose as children ranging in age from 10 to 15 years old and wait for predators to approach them for conversation. PeeJ methods are supported by the Department of Justice as well as local law enforcement agencies. This line of research proves valuable as it exposes tactics used by predators, helps policymakers counter predators with appropriate preventative courses of action, educates the public regarding the manipulation techniques used to lure children on and offline, and helps children understand how to protect themselves. References

The Effects of Organizational and Community Context on Local of CSEC Prevalence, Prosecution of Computer Child Pornography Cases., and Services is a project designed by awardee, Fund for the City of New York. The award has a start date of 9/1/2009 and an end date of 2/28/2012. The Center for Court Innovation proposes to collaborate with Richard Curtis, Kirk Dombrowski, and Bilal Khan to conduct a national study that would: (1) estimate the size and scope of the commercial sexual exploitation of children (CSEC); (2) describe the characteristics and needs of CSEC victims; (3) explore available services; and (4) analyze prosecution outcomes for victims and exploiters. The populations of interest would include youth under 18 who are engaged in prostitution, child pornography, or related CSEC activities and those who are controlling or profiting from them.

Buzzell, T.

Criminal Justice Studies, vol. 20, no. 4, pp. 391-405, 2007.

Abstract: This study examines how U.S. prosecutors deal with the problem of child pornography as a facet of computer crime. Results from the 2001 National Prosecutors Survey reveal that the likelihood of prosecuting this form of crime increases with having a budget for experts, using alternatives to prosecution, and working in districts with higher crime rates and higher levels of income. Context therefore matters in the prosecution of computer child pornography cases. Further research is necessary, however, to understand how prosecutors handle advanced forms of child sexual exploitation.

Mandatory Reporting of Childhood Sexual Abuse in Israel: What Happens After the Report? Oz, Sheri; Balshan, Dorit.

Journal of Child Sexual Abuse, vol. 16, no. 4, pp. 1 - 22, 2007.

Abstract: This study outlined issues of mandatory reporting of child sexual abuse, and the inconsistency of post-report interventions in Israel on children and their families. This paper suggests amendments to the mandatory reporting laws in Israel to better protect all children from sexual exploitation while providing consistent and expert professional intervention. Although studies have been conducted regarding the impact of mandated reporting laws on professionals, there is a scarcity of research exploring the impact on families and children affected by mandated reporting. There are several problems regarding mandatory reporting of suspected child abuse in Israel, namely the differences between sexual abuse and other forms of abuse that need to be addressed; far fewer allegations of sexual abuse are substantiated in a court of law than physical abuse or neglect. The tendency of some countries to advocate legal interventions for sexual abuse and therapeutic interventions for other forms of abuse may stem from emotional reactions to sexual abuse rather than the effectiveness of the legal approach. Therefore, sexual abuse should be dealt with using a separate law geared to handle the special nature of sexual abuse that warrants unique expertise on the part of the professional involved, namely an amendment to the law that requires reporting of all cases of suspected sexual abuse regardless of the age of the abuser and the relationship with the victim. So that the mandatory reporting can be an instrument of change, the separate law should clearly stipulate the procedures to be followed after the report has been made and should state the minimal qualifications of an expert in the field of sexual abuse. Future research should include two major issues: the factors associated with disclosure of abuse and the child s expectations, and the consequences of the disclosure for both the child and family members upon implementation of the ensuing legal and/or clinical interventions, including possible differential effects over the long and short terms. Figure, references

Problematic Internet Experiences: Primary Or Secondary Presenting Problems In Persons Seeking Mental Health Care?

Mitchell, Kimberly J.; Wells, Melissa.

Social Science and Medicine, vol. 65, pp. 1136-1141, Sept. 2007.

Abstract: This study utilizes data from clinical reports of 1441 youth and adults in the USA to examine the types of problematic Internet experiences mental health professionals report as clients' primary or secondary presenting problems. Overall, clients who present in treatment with an Internet problem are more likely to have problems related to overuse of the Internet; use of adult pornography; use of child pornography; sexual exploitation perpetration; and gaming, gambling, or role-playing. Other Internet-related problems, such as isolative-avoidant use, sexual exploitation victimization, harassment perpetration, and online infidelity were equally likely to present in treatment as a primary problem or secondary to other mental health concerns. Some differences between youth and adult clients were also identified. Findings suggest some initial support for the importance of including Internet use, experiences, and behavior as part of an initial clinical assessment.

Youth Sexual Exploitation on the Internet: DSM-IV Diagnoses and Gender Differences in Co- Occurring Mental Health Issues.

Wells, M. and Mitchell, K.

Child and Adolescent Social Work Journal, 24(3), pp. 235-260, 2007.

Abstract: This paper explores conventional (non-Internet-related) mental health issues and DSMIV diagnoses seen among a sample of 512 youth receiving mental health services for an Internet- related problem, with particular attention to victims of online sexual exploitation. Youth victims of online sexual exploitation were more likely to have a post-traumatic stress disorder than youth with other Internet-related problems. Specific attention was given to differences among subgroups of female and male youth victims of online sexual exploitation as compared with same-gender youth with other Internet-related problems. Findings suggest the importance of including Internet use and victimization as part of a standard clinical assessment.

Gender-Based Violence Against Children In Emergencies: Save the Children UK's Response. Hyder, Tina; Veigh, Johanna Mac.

Gender and Development, vol. 15, no. 1, pp. 8 1-93, Mar 2007.

Abstract: Violence against children is a global phenomenon. During humanitarian crises, and armed conflict in particular, the potential for gender-based violence (GBV), including sexual exploitation, increases. Children, particularly adolescent girls, are vulnerable. This article traces the impact of an expose of sexual abuse by humanitarian workers on the wider protection policies and practices of Save the Children UK. The article concludes that awareness of gender discrimination must underpin the implementation of protection policies for all children and their carers. Furthermore, it proposes that comprehensive responses to GBV must be devised, alongside prevention strategies, if children are to be effectively protected. Adapted from the source document.

Are We Protecting Our Youth Online? An Examination of Programs Keeping Youth Safe and Analysis of Policy Vacuum.

Marcum, Catherine.

International Journal of Cyber Criminology, vol. 1, no. 2, pp. 198 - 212, 2007.

Abstract: After reviewing some of the risks of criminal victimization confronting youth who use the Internet, this paper describes the theoretical basis and effectiveness of strategies to prevent the online victimization of youth, and the author suggests some situational-based crime prevention strategies based on empirical evidence. Youth who use the Internet regularly risk being exposed to sexual solicitation, unwanted harassment, and unwanted exposure to sexual material. The Federal Government has made numerous attempts to pass legislation and initiate protective programs that will prevent the online victimization of youth. This paper briefly reviews those Federal statutes that have targeted various harmful online activities but that have been overturned by Federal courts as unconstitutional. Recently, the U.S. Congress has had some success in passing legislation that protects adolescents from online victimization while they are at school. There have also been efforts to mount proactive law enforcement efforts aimed at reducing online victimization. In addition to legislation, the Federal Government has developed various programs that assist law enforcement and parents in protecting children online. The Internet Crimes against Children (ICAC) Task Force Program, developed by the U.S. Justice Department's Office of Juvenile Justice and Delinquency Prevention (OJJDP) in 1998, aimed to help State and local law enforcement agencies create programs that target online enticement and child pornography. One of the more successful programs, CyberTipline and CyberTipline II provide for citizens to report suspicious activity on the Internet. Based on such citizen reports, more than 550 individuals have been arrested for child sexual exploitation, and 627 search warrants have been served. Programs that increase guardianship for youth in their online activities while decreasing their risk of exposure to predators (i.e. digital locks and protections), as well as deter the motivated offender from approaching youth online, should decrease the likelihood of victimization. 62 references.

Online Requests for Sexual Pictures from Youth: Risk factors and Incident Characteristics. Mitchell, K. J., Finkelhor, D., and Wolak, J.

Journal of Adolescent Health, 41, pp. 196-203, 2007.

Abstract: Purpose: The aim of this study was to explore the prevalence and characteristics of youth who receive requests to make and send sexual pictures of themselves over the Internet. Methods: Data were collected as part of the Second Youth Internet Safety Survey, a nationally representative telephone survey of 1,500 youth Internet users, ages 10–17 years, in the United States. Results: Among Internet-using youth 4% reported an online request to send a sexual picture of themselves during the previous year. Only one youth of 65 sample case subjects actually complied. Being female, being of Black ethnicity, having a close online relationship, engaging in sexual behavior online, and experiencing physical or sexual abuse offline were risk factors for receiving a request for a sexual picture. Incidents that involved requests for sexual pictures were more likely to occur when youth were in the presence of friends, communicating with an adult, someone they met online, who had sent a sexual picture to the youth, and who attempted or made some form of offline contact with the youth.

Assisting Children Born of Sexual Exploitation and Abuse.

Rumble, Lauren; Mehta, Swati B.

Forced Migration Review, Mar2007, Issue 27, pp. 20-2 1, 1 color.

Abstract The article deals with the strategy issued by the United Nations (UN) Secretary-General to support victims of sexual exploitation and abuse by UN staff. The strategy includes a controversial proposal to introduce DNA sampling for all UN staff. A Task Force on Protection from Sexual Exploitation and Abuse in Humanitarian Crises was established by the Inter-Agency Standing Committee and a report was published setting out the principles of a code of conduct for humanitarian workers.

Factors Vitiating Against the Effectiveness of the Nigeria Police in Combating the Criminal Exploitation of Children and Women.

Elechi, O. O.; Okosun, T. Y.; Ngwe, J. E.

African Journal of Criminology and Justice Studies, vol. 3, no. 1, pp. 1-49, 2007.

Abstract: This article examines the challenges facing Nigeria's law enforcement in the effort to limit criminal exploitation of children and women. Nigeria is considered a major source and destination for the trafficking of persons for the purposes of sexual work, adoption, labor, and sale of body parts. The present article argues that several factors lead to limited effectiveness for the Nigeria police. These factors include inadequate policing, corruption, deprivation of freedoms, social injustices, few social opportunities, conflicting social values, gender imbalance in education and work, and weak social institutions. In order to address this complex problem, global and local combating strategies are discussed. At the international level, there should be improvements in framework and knowledge regarding trafficking. Locally, the six primary issues that must be addressed are corruption, inadequate social control, poverty, gender inequality, the plight of globalization, and labor opportunities. Short-term goals should focus on education about the problem of trafficking, whereas long-term policy must address the fundamental social and economic conditions that permit trafficking to occur.

The Health and Well-Being of Neglected, Abused and Exploited Children: The Kyiv Street Children Project.

Kerfoot, Michael; Koshyl, Vira; Roganov, Oleksandr; Mikhailichenko, Kateryna; Gorbova, Irina; Pottage, David.

Child Abuse and Neglect, Jan. 2007, Vol. 31 Issue 1, pp. 27-37.

Abstract: Objective: To report on the backgrounds and physical and emotional well-being of street children using two street shelters in Kyiv, Ukraine. This study is important because personal accounts of street children may highlight individual or family factors that are associated with vulnerability for and risk of poor mental health, and these could have serious repercussions for the future. This study also poses a challenge to research because street children are a highly elusive population that services find hard to reach. Methods: Ninety-seven children were recruited and interviewed using a semistructured, psychosocial interview schedule; psychopathology was measured using the Strengths and Difficulties Questionnaire (SDQ) and the Mood and Feelings Questionnaire (MFQ). Results: Seventy percent of street children scored for behavioral and emotional difficulties on the SDQ, and 74% scored for depression on the MFQ. Current health problems were reported by 78%, with 43% described as persistent or severe. Two thirds of the children in this sample were not homeless but had chosen life on the streets in preference to permanent residence with their families. Their "survival" history on the streets contributed to the development of three different profiles of vulnerability. Conclusions: High rates of physical and emotional problems in a population of street children, many of whom were still connected to their families, emphasize the importance of developing different approaches for children with different vulnerabilities. This study also demonstrates the feasibility of embedding on-going field research into the service dimension of "front-line" social care agencies.

Cyberspace and Child Abuse Images: A Feminist Perspective.
Harrison, C.
Affilia, vol. 21, no. 4, pp. 365-379, 2006.

Abstract: This article approaches cyberspace as a socially constructed space in which gendered power relations are replicated and examines how cyberspace has been expropriated to escalate child sexual abuse and other sexual offenses. Making connections between different forms of abuse of women and children demonstrates that feminist perspectives provide an essential framework for understanding how new information and communication technologies are reinforcing attitudes that degrade and dehumanize women and children. Analyzing the relationship between gender and other oppressions challenges the hegemony of discourses that emphasize freedom and the democratizing potential of cyberspace and shows how cyberspace is a site for increased violence and exploitation of women and children.

Children in Sex, Adults in Crime: Constructing and Confining Teens.
Raby, Rebecca.
Resources for Feminist Research/Documentation sur la Recherche Feministe, vol. 31, no. 3-4, pp. 9-28, 2006.

Abstract: This paper explores two pieces of legislation proposed in Ontario in 2001, the Rescuing Children from Sexual Exploitation Act and the No-More-Free-Ride for Young Offenders Act, in order to examine how young people are alternatively defined as children and as adults due to current constructs of childhood, adolescence, adulthood, and victimhood. Adapted from the source document.

Sheldon Kennedy and a Canadian Tragedy Revisited: A Comparative Look at U.S. and Canadian Jurisprudence on Youth Sports Organizations' Civil Liability for Child Sexual Exploitation. Preston, M. Bradford.
Vanderbilt Journal of Transnational Law, Oct. 2006, Vol. 39 Issue 4, pp. 1333-1372.

Abstract: National Hockey League player Sheldon Kennedy's 1997 revelation that his award-winning junior hockey coach had molested him for years created a national outcry in Canada. It resulted in the appointment of a special commission and declarations from the United States and Canada that this must never happen again. However, Kennedy was not alone; child sexual exploitation occurs at the hands of youth coaches across geographic and class boundaries and across individual and team sports. Youth sports organizations, including schools, have approached the human and legal issues presented by child sexual exploitation in numerous ways. This Note analyzes the differences between--and strengths and weaknesses of--U.S. and Canadian courts' respective treatment of these organizations' actions both before and after sexual abuse is discovered. It also examines the degree to which youth sports organizations in both nations have acted to prevent future problems, specifically as compared to the recommendations of the commission formed in response to Kennedy's story. The Author concludes the Canadian judicial standard for youth sports organizations' liability ultimately is superior to the standard employed by U.S. courts.

Boys Are Not Sexually Exploited?: A Challenge to Practitioners.

Lillywhite, Ralph; Skidmore, Paula.

Child Abuse Review, vol. 15, no. 5, pp. 351 - 361, September-October 2006.

Abstract: This paper argues that the view that boys are not sexually exploited is very common among many professionals in the United Kingdom working with young men and reasons for this belief and reasons for this mindset to change. The issue of boys and young men at risk of sexual exploitation is slowly being recognized by practitioners and more services are expanding their provision to ensure support and facilities are open to boys and young men at risk, as well as girls and young women. This is just the beginning of reducing and preventing sexual exploitation of male children. Until all professionals working with vulnerable young men ask themselves, is this young man being sexually exploited, young men are going to remain hidden and unsupported. This paper draws on evidence collected from Barnardo’s Young Men s Project (BYMP) which provides free and confidential services aimed at preventing and reducing sexual exploitation of male children. BYMP is a London-wide service working with boys under 18 who are experiencing or are vulnerable to sexual exploitation. History and practice have in the past suggested that boys and young men are at no, or low, risk of sexual exploitation. This paper argues that this is impossible to conclude with such a weak knowledge base concerning the extent and nature of sexual exploitation of male children in the United Kingdom.

Child Sexual Exploitation: A Partnership Response and Model Intervention.

Leblock, Evelyn Kerrigan; King, Siobhan.

Child Abuse Review, vol. 15, no. 5, pp. 362-372, Sept-Oct 2006.

Abstract: The fact of child sexual exploitation is well-known by youth services, but many fail to recognize the vulnerability of children to this abuse even among those presenting with obvious related damage. By the time they become adolescents, they present a challenge to intervention even among the most experienced youth professionals. A model of identification of such children and subsequent risk assessment and intervention developed by a statutory/voluntary partnership between the Camden (London) Social Services Dept and the north London Barnardo's Young Women's Project is described. The Children Abused through Sexual Exploitation (CATSE) project was established in 1999 to recognize cases of child sexual exploitation (or prostitution), treat the child as a victim of abuse, safeguard such children, work to prevent abuse and help children recover from victimization, and prosecute those responsible. The procedures, methods, and outcomes of the CATSE project are discussed.

Meetings the Needs of Sexually Exploited Young People: The Challenge of Conducting Policy- Relevant Research.

Scott, Sara; Harper, Zoe.

Child Abuse Review, vol. 15, no. 5, pp. 313 - 325, September-October 2006.

Abstract: This paper presents findings from a research study which explored the extent of, and responses to, the service needs of young people at risk of sexual exploitation in London, England. The research study had a relatively high profile during the 2 years it was being conducted and the interviews themselves inevitably raised awareness of the issues regarding the sexual exploitation of young people. Even though recommendations of the research study were supported by the Metropolitan Police, the Association of London Government, the Greater London Authority, and the Corporation of London, the Baroness Scotland made it clear that the Government had no plans to follow the report's recommendation to remove the provision to prosecute young people who are considered to persistently and voluntarily return to prostitution. However, indications were seen of the research s immediate value in relation to both policy and service development. The London Child Protection Committee has produced a draft pan-London protocol for working with children who are sexually exploited and has held a consultation seminar. The Bridge House Trust has funded the development of a new specialist service in south London. It provides a service in some of the highest risk boroughs identified in the research and also provides consultancy and training to those boroughs not served by the specialist service, but identified as in need. Meeting the needs of sexually exploited young people in London was commissioned by the Bridge House Trust and the research was undertaken by researchers from Barnardo's Policy and Research Unit. This paper outlines the findings of a 2 year study exploring the extent of, and responses to, the service needs of young people at risk of sexual exploitation in London, England. It was a case study in conducting policy-relevant research into a hidden social problem. Data were collected through interviews with key professionals across London.

Participation And Young People Involved In Prostitution.

Brown, Kate.

Child Abuse Review, Sep/Oct2006, Vol. 15 Issue 5, p.294-312.

Abstract: This paper discusses a campaign which involves young people with experience of prostitution in influencing policy and practice which affects this group: the National Youth Campaign on Sexual Exploitation (the Youth Campaign). It is argued that participation is critical to improving outcomes for young people involved in prostitution, yet is often overlooked. Through participation, young people with experience of prostitution can build their self-esteem whilst also helping agencies and policy makers develop more effective strategies on youth prostitution. The paper examines in detail one piece of work undertaken by the Youth Campaign: a workshop run by two young women at a national conference on sexual exploitation. In addition, it gives an overview of current research, policy and practice on participation and young people involved in prostitution and makes recommendations for how practice in this area could be improved.

Criminal Exploitation of Women and Children and the Important Role of Community Policing. Murray, John.

Police Practice and Research, May2006, Vol. 7 Issue 2, p.125-134.

Abstract: Australia, like all other responsible countries, considers the sexual exploitation of women and children an abhorrent criminal act and accordingly regards this activity as a priority public policy issue. Consistent with the UN protocols, Australia has committed considerable resources to the pursuit of offenders and has in place severe penalties. Relentless pursuit of offenders is critical but this paper draws attention to the emphasis the UN has placed on identifying the women and children as 'victims' and the consequent need to provide them with the rights, privileges, and due sensitivities that we afford victims of other crimes. The context in which policing takes place has, arguably, changed since 'September 11.' Some police services have tended to move away from community policing and return to the traditional model of policing. For the prevention and detection of crimes like sexual exploitation this is seen as a counter-productive move. Traditional policing distances police from the rest of the community— while it is difficult for police to gain mutual respect and trust with the community for conventional crimes, the unique nature of sexual exploitation places additional challenges on police which are best met by maintaining community policing, its fine ethical principles and its practical resolve.

Trafficking In Women and Children (Part 2): Strategies and Responses.
Egan, R.
Community Safety Journal, vol. 5, no. 2, pp. 14-16, 2006.

Abstract: This second part of a literature review on the trafficking of women and children for sexual exploitation examines some policy responses to the problem and the dilemmas faced by practitioners. There are a number of strategies and tactics adopted by different countries in tackling trafficking. The direction of these policies depends on the emphasis determined by the political concerns involved. Overall, four guidelines first introduced at the 2004 International Police Executive Symposium should be added to the U.N. Convention Against Transnational Organised Crime and its Protocols. Although they have yet to be adopted, these are sound organizing principles that should also be reflected in local partnership strategies.

Reuniting Fractured Families After a Disaster: The Role of the National Center for Missing & Exploited Children.

Broughton, Daniel D.; Allen, Ernest E.; Hannemann, Robert E.; Petrikin, Joshua E. Pediatrics, May2006 Supplement, Vol. 117, p. S442-S445.

Abstract: The article focuses on the role of the U.S. National Center for Missing & Exploited Children (NCMEC) in reuniting families who were dislocated by the landfall of Hurricane Katrina in New Orleans, Louisiana in 2005. Records show how efficient NCMEC is in locating missing children and reuniting them with their families. It implements systems and programs designed to search for missing children in different locales. When Hurricane Katrina devastated New Orleans, children where dislocated from their families. NCMEC created programs specifically to aid in reuniting the families, such as a hotline with a unique toll-free number and a collaboration with law enforcement officers. It also used the opportunity to emphasized the importance of creating a family emergency plan.

The Sexual Exploitation of Children in Mexico.

Azaola, Elena.

Police Practice and Research, May2006, Vol. 7 Issue 2, p. 97-110, 3 charts.

Abstract: This paper describes research conducted into the commercial sexual exploitation of children in Mexico. It describes the economic circumstances that give rise to the phenomenon and provides an estimation of the numbers of children in seven cities in Mexico. The nature and methods of the exploiters are described and recommendations are made for improvements in law, practice, and procedure to tackle the problem.

The Flesh Trade in Europe: Trafficking in Women and Children for the Purpose of Commercial Sexual Exploitation.

Melrose, Margaret; Barrett, David.

Police Practice and Research, May2006, Vol. 7 Issue 2, p. 111-123.

Abstract: This paper explores the phenomenon of trafficking for the purpose of commercial sexual exploitation (C SE) in the context of a changing Europe and pays particular attention to the situation in the UK. It discusses difficulties with defining the issue of trafficking and the reasons for an apparent increase in this phenomenon in recent years. It then considers trafficking as a process and the challenges of measuring the scale of the problem. The paper goes on to consider trafficking routes and examines the situation in Britain. Finally, official responses to the problem in Britain are considered.

An Overwhelming Sense of Injustice? An Exploration of Child Sexual Abuse in Relation to the Concept of Justice.

Green, Lorraine.

Critical Social Policy, vol. 26, no. 1, pp. 74-100, Feb 2006.

Abstract: This article explores the relationship between justice and child sexual abuse, developing a broader theoretical conception of justice than that customarily applied. The traditional legal perception of justice as the attempted prosecution of alleged perpetrators is widened to encompass justice as initial prevention of abuse, the fair treatment of children by the criminal justice and child protection systems, and the subsequent after-care and compensation of abused children and adults. Concepts of justice are therefore examined within a chronological lifecourse trajectory, as well as being extended from traditional notions of due process and desert including understandings of justice as human rights, 'fair shares' and liberation. Particular social constructions of childhood are revealed to be highly significant regarding how justice is perceived and operationalized. Therefore, the interaction between perceptions of justice and responses to child sexual abuse is examined, relative to wider understandings of childhood.

Exploiting West Africa's Children: Trafficking, Slavery and Uneven Development. Manzo, Kate.

Area, Dec2005, Vol. 37 Issue 4, p.393-401, 3 charts.

Abstract: This paper analyses child trafficking and slavery in relation to media coverage of West African children, international law and academic research within geography and development studies. The meaning and practice of child trafficking is examined in the context of related debates about child labour, exploitation and uneven development. The analysis highlights key differences between trafficking and slavery, thereby illuminating the varying forms of exploitation at work in different relations of power.

Trafficking in Children for the Purpose of Sexual Exploitation in the EU.

Staiger, Ines.

European Journal of Crime, Criminal Law and Criminal Justice, 2005, Vol. 13 Issue 4, p.603624.

Abstract This article looks at developments concerning trafficking in children for the purpose of sexual exploitation in the European Union, focusing on the European Commission's Council Framework Decision of July 19, 2002 on combating trafficking in human beings. Article 1 of the framework defines tracking in children for purpose of sexual exploitation. At the heart of it stands the trafficking operation. This covers recruitment, transportation, transfer, harboring and subsequent reception of the child. An underlying goal of the trafficking process is the sexual exploitation of the trafficked child. Another goal is the approximation of criminal sanctions. In summary, the framework does provide for requirements to facilitate the prosecution of trafficking in children but it does not adequately follow such objective with regard to criminal sanctions.

Acceptable Victims? Sexually Exploited Youth in the U.S.

Lloyd, Rachel.

Encounter, Autumn 2005, Vol. 18 Issue 3, pp. 6-18.

Abstract: The article focuses on the sexual exploitation of children in the U.S. in September 2005. A study conducted in 2001 states that hundreds of thousands of adolescents are sexually exploited annually in the U.S. Several factors have been cited as the cause of youth prostitution. The media also has a role in the celebrity-like status bestowed upon pimps and exploiters. National advocates indicate that the prostitution of adolescents is rampant in New York City.

Violence and Exploitation of Children in Tajikistan.

Haarr, Robin.

Central Asian Survey, Jun2005, Vol. 24 Issue 2, pp. 13 1-149.

Abstract Analyzes the phenomenon of violence and exploitation of children in Tajikistan. Violence as defined by the WHO Report on Violence and Health; Government statistics on violence and exploitation of children; Social science research on the subject; Requirements for achieving the progressive implementation of the Convention on the Rights of the Child.

International Trafficking In Children: Will New U.S Legislation Provide An Ending To The Story?

Mathews, Stacey.

Houston Journal of International Law, Spring 2005, Vol. 27 Issue 3, pp. 649-702.

Abstract: Focuses on the growing problem with sexual exploitation and child trafficking. Requirement for a multinational response with international coordination of law enforcement to address the problem; Consideration of poverty as another root of trafficking and child prostitution; Role played by organized crime in many countries where trafficking occurs.

Trafficking of Women and Children for Exploitation in the Commercial Sex Trade: The Case of the Russian Federation.

Orlova, Alexandra V.

Georgetown Journal of Gender and the Law, Symposium Issue 2005, Vol. 6 Issue 2, pp.157-178.

Abstract This article focuses on trafficking of women and children for exploitation in the commercial sex trade. The trafficking of human beings for exploitation in the commercial sex trade is not a new phenomenon. Trafficking has been endemic in South and Southeast Asia for decades. However, relatively recent changes in the global economy account for both the increase in human trafficking as well as trafficking from a variety of new "source" countries, including countries with transitional economies that were created after the collapse of the Soviet Union. Russia in particular has experienced, and continues to experience, a "regional crisis" in trafficking. The difficulties in dealing with the problem of human trafficking are exacerbated by the absence of consensus over a definition of this phenomenon. Various governmental and nongovernmental bodies that deal with human trafficking define it differently. Some agencies are only concerned with trafficking that is transnational in scope, disregarding regional and intranational manifestations of this problem.

Commercial and Sexual Exploitation of Children and Young People in the UK—A Review. Chase, Elaine; Statham, June.

Child Abuse Review, Jan/Feb2005, Vol. 14 Issue 1, pp. 4-25.

Abstract: This paper reviews recent information and data relevant to the commercial sexual exploitation of children and young people in the UK. Three main aspects of exploitation are addressed: abuse through prostitution; abuse through pornography; and the trafficking of children and young people to and through the UK for the purposes of commercial sexual exploitation. Most published research in this area relates to young people exploited through prostitution. The review explores the range of vulnerability factors, the processes used to engage young people in prostitution and the types of support strategies for those being exploited. Rather less information is currently available on the scale of child pornography, or the links between the use of pornography and other forms of sexual abuse. The internet as a modern technology for proliferating child pornography is discussed, alongside its role in providing opportunities for paedophiles to access and 'groom' children for sexual purposes. Finally, the review provides a summary of research on trafficking of children to and through the UK for the purposes of commercial sexual exploitation and demonstrates the limited knowledge about this topic.

Human Trafficking in East Asia: Current Trends, Data Collection, and Knowledge Gaps. Lee, June J. H.

International Migration, 2005, Vol. 43 Issue 1/2, pp. 165-201.

Abstract: Focuses on the movement of people and volume of migration flows in East Asia. Focus on trafficking in women and children for sexual exploitation and highlight serious violations of human rights; Examination of the general trends in human trafficking; Factors contributing to the rapid growth of a market-driven intraregional migration.

Preventing Sexual Exploitation of Children and Teens.

Iton, Anthony; Oliver, Mary Margaret; Torgensen, Kirk.

Journal of Law, Medicine and Ethics, Winter2005 Supplement, Vol. 33 Issue 4, pp.38-39.

Abstract The article presents the views of some conference participants concerning sexual exploitation of children and teens in the U. S. One conference moderator noted that the problems of sexual exploitation involves law enforcement, social services and health organizations and the advocacy groups. Another speaker called the attention of political entities to focus on cases of child exploitation.

Financial Exploitation of the Sexuality of Migrant Children in Greece.

Antonopoulos, Georgios A.

Crime and Justice International, vol. 20, no. 83, pp. 19 - 22, November/ December 2004.

Abstract: This article provides a brief overview of the financial exploitation of the sexuality of migrant children in the country of Greece and combative measures to address this exploitation. Since the beginning of the 1990's, Greece has experienced a large influx of migrants which include: Albanians, Bulgarians, Georgians, Romanians, Russians, and Ukrainians. This influx of migrants has created the exploitation of migrant children, who are being trafficked for a variety of purposes, such as sexual exploitation. According to a recent study, about 7.5 percent (1,005) of the average 13,400 individuals who were trafficked annually from 1990 to 2000 in Greece were children with the majority of the children coming from Albania. The methods for recruiting children include: abduction, selling protection to unaccompanied children crossing the Greek-Albanian border, purchase from family and/or relatives, false marriage proposal, false promise of work, and exploitation by members of the family. Those measures undertaken to combat the trafficking of children usually fall within the context of measures undertaken against the trafficking in human beings in general. There are international initiatives taken among the members of the United Nations, the European Union, and others, as well as local and national measures. In addition, the new Law 3064 of 2002 includes harsher penalties for traffickers of children. References

"Don't Trust Me With Your Child": Non-Legal Precautions When the Law Cannot Prevent Sexual Exploitation in Youth Sports.

Peterson, Jamie.

Texas Review of Entertainment and Sports Law, Spring 2004, Vol. 5 Issue 2, pp. 297-323.

Abstract: Discusses laws aimed at preventing and remedying child exploitation by youth coaches, with a particular focus on Texas law. Reasons behind the difficulties for a sexually abused athlete to achieve full civil remedy; Proponents and opponents of coaching background checks; Non-legal methods for the prevention of sexual exploitation of child-athletes.

The Sexual and Mental Health Problems of Street Children: A Transcultural Preventative Approach in Counselling Psychology.

Guernina, Zoubida.

Counselling Psychology Quarterly; 17 (1) Mar 2004, pp. 99-105.

Abstract: Sexual and mental health problems are on the increase world-wide especially among street children. A high proportion of vulnerable children who live in the street suffer exploitation, poor quality of life that often lead to sexual and mental health problems. Evidence is needed on the theoretical perspectives taken to address the existing gaps in counselling psychology research and practice on the plight of street children. It is also important to identify interventions that could be implemented to prevent the expansion of sexual and mental health problems among street children. Because of paucity of evidence in counselling psychology, an attempt has been made to highlight the risks factors associated with street children such as sexual exploitation, engaging in unsafe sex at an early age, promiscuity, unplanned pregnancy which tend to lead to mental health problems. Case studies are presented that illustrate the importance of a preventative transcultural approach in counselling psychology.

U.S. Domestic Prosecution of the American International Sex Tourist.

Andrews, Sara K.

Journal of Criminal Law and Criminology, Winter2004, Vol. 94 Issue 2, pp. 415-454.

Abstract The article highlights the efforts of the U.S. to protect children from sexual exploitation as of 2003. The commercial sexual exploitation of minors by international tourists is a humanitarian tragedy carried out on a grand scale with virtually no repercussions for the criminal perpetrators. Over the past decade, the U.S. has publicly recognized the severity of the problem of child sexual exploitation on a global level and has undertaken measures designed to help solve the problem. In June 2002, the U.S. House of Representatives passed the Sex Tourism Prohibition Improvement Act of

2002, declaring the bill would close significant loopholes in the existing law. Through its legislative efforts and support for the Optional Protocol, the U.S. has taken steps to acknowledge the gravity of the global problem of child sexual exploitation, as well as the complicity of U.S. citizens in its perpetuation. However, recognition of the severity of the problem, although an important development, is only the first step in the process of addressing child sexual exploitation in a meaningful and effective way. Since its passage in 1994, the Child Sexual Abuse Prevention Act has resulted in few actual prosecutions of U.S. nationals who traveled abroad for the purpose of committing sex crimes against minors.

Internet-initiated Sex Crimes Against Minors: Implications for Prevention Based on Findings from a National Study.

Wolak, J., Finkelhor, D., and Mitchell, K. J.

Journal of Adolescent Health, 35, 424.e1 1–424.e20, 2004.

Abstract: Purpose: To describe the characteristics of episodes in which juveniles became victims of sex crimes committed by people they met through the Internet. Methods: A national survey of a stratified random sample of 2574 law enforcement agencies conducted between October 2001 and July 2002. Telephone interviews were conducted with local, state, and federal law enforcement investigators concerning 129 sexual offenses against juvenile victims that originated with online encounters. Results: Victims in these crimes were primarily 13- through 15-year-old teenage girls (75%) who met adult offenders (76% older than 25) in Internet chat rooms. Most offenders did not deceive victims about the fact that they were adults who were interested in sexual relationships. Most victims met and had sex with the adults on more than one occasion. Half of the victims were described as being in love with or feeling close bonds with the offenders. Almost all cases with male victims involved male offenders. Offenders used violence in 5% of the episodes.

Sexual Crimes against and Exploitation of Children and the Law in Papua New Guinea.

Luluaki, John Y.

International Journal of Law, Policy and the Family, vol. 17, no. 3, pp. 275-307, Dec 2003.

Abstract: On 28 Mar 2002, the National Parliament of Papua New Guinea (PNG) passed the Criminal Code (Sexual Offences and Crimes Against Children) Act (the new law). Its purpose was to repeal certain sections and amend others of the Criminal Code, Ch. 262 (the Code) dealing with sexual offenses against children to reflect more appropriately the changed and changing circumstances of sexual violence against women and children in the country. The old Criminal Code provisions relating to sexual offenses against children and women generally went under the legislative scalpel changing completely the landscape of the old provisions with this enactment. The purpose of this article is to discuss the different provisions contained in the new law dealing with the issue of sexual crimes against children. This is done in the context of both legislative reform of outdated criminal laws and PNG's international obligation to safeguard children from all forms of abuse and exploitation and protect the rights of children. 9 References. Adapted from the source document.

The Legacy of the Clergy Abuse Scandal.
Finkelhor, David.
Child Abuse and Neglect; 27 (11) Nov 2003, pp.1225-1229.
Abstract: The clergy abuse scandal in the Catholic Church has left its mark on child protection efforts. It was a major national story about child maltreatment that has dominated the media for more than a year, prompting discussions about child exploitation issues in countless homes and organizations. Asks whether it has ultimately helped the cause of child protection and concludes that the controversy has had a complex kind of impact in the United States, both positive and negative.

Commercial Sexual Exploitation of Youth the South Africa.
Snell, Cudore L.
Journal of Negro Education, Fall2003, Vol. 72 Issue 4, pp. 506-514.
Abstract: This article provides an overview of commercial exploitation, with a focus on commercial sexual exploitation of Black children and youth in South Africa. A literature review on research on the labor exploitation among youth globally and in South Africa and on the commercial sexual exploitation of South African youth is presented first. International and national policy proclamations related to South African youth are highlighted. Second, findings from a study of Black South African youth who engaged in commercial sexual activities in Cape Town are presented. Third, conclusions and recomm-endations to consider the complex social, educational, economic, and political aspects of child exploitation are offered. This includes implications for further research, policy, and programs to assist this group of youth and their families.

Sexual Abuse, Family Violence, and Female Delinquency: Findings from a Longitudinal Study.

Herrera, Veronica M.; McCloskey, Laura Ann.

Violence and Victims, vol. 18, no. 3, pp. 3 19-334, June 2003.

Abstract: The current study examines the effects of three forms of childhood victimization on self-reported delinquency and aggression in adolescent girls. These analyses are based on a longitudinal sample of 141 mother-daughter pairs participating in a study about marital violence and child development. When the children were school aged, mothers and children provided reports describing (1) child exposure to marital violence, (2) escalated physical abuse against the child, and (c) child sexual abuse. Children were followed up into adolescence and reinterviewed. Self-reports of delinquency (violent and nonviolent), running away, and violence against parents were collected. Results indicate that out of the three forms of victimization, child sexual abuse emerged as the strongest predictor of girls' violent and nonviolent criminal behavior. Girls with a history of physical abuse in childhood were most likely to assault their parents. Witnessing marital violence failed to contribute further to delinquency, beyond the adverse association with childhood sexual abuse. Findings highlight a unique avenue for delinquency in girls via childhood sexual exploitation. 8 Tables, 34 References.

In: Child Exploitation Prevention and Interdiction ISBN: 978-1-61122-854-0
Editor: Andrew K. Clampet

Chapter 2

FUNDED RESEARCH*

Library of Congress/National Institute of Justice

A National Study of Internet-Facilitated Commercial Sexual Exploitation of Children (IF-CSEC) in the Criminal Justice System is a project designed by the awardee, the University of New Hampshire. The award has a start date of 1/1/2007 and end date of 12/31/2009. This study of Internet-facilitated CSEC (IF-CSEC) crimes focuses on the future directions of commercial sexual exploitation of children and youth by looking at how offenders use the Internet to facilitate CSEC in a broad range of cases handled by law enforcement agencies, including child prostitution, trafficking, sex tourism, child pornography and other CSEC crimes. It brings together an experienced research partner with a strong research background in child sexual exploitation, the Crimes against Children Research Center, and a law enforcement partner with a high degree of expertise in the use of Internet technology in sexual exploitation crimes, the Internet Crimes Against Children Task Forces.

Research into the Scope, Investigation, and Prosecution of Technology-Facilitated Child Exploitation: the 3rd National Online Victimization Study is a project designed by the awardee, University of New Hampshire. The award has a start date of 7/1/2009 and an end date of 6/30/20 12. This study is designed to help law enforcement combat technology-facilitated child

* This is an edited, reformatted and augmented edition of a joint report compiled by the Library of Congress and National Institute of Justice.

exploitation crimes. It will gather detailed national data on a number of policy and practice relevant topics including: 1) new developments and numerical trends in cases coming to law enforcement attention; 2) what investigative strategies are associated with more favorable outcomes; 3) what challenges and dilemmas confront prosecutors; 4) what indicators and investigative procedures are more likely to identify child pornography offenders who have also committed crimes against or endangered children in their environments; and 5) how investigators are managing and responding to cases of sexual images produced and disseminated by youth. The data will be gathered using a proven, successful methodology, a 2-stage survey of a national sample of law enforcement agencies that will include interviews with investigators and prosecutors involved in a representative sample of more than 1000 technology-facilitated crimes.

National Study of Internet and Technology-Facilitated Risks to Youth is a project designed by the awardee, University of New Hampshire. The award has a start date of 7/1/2009 and an end date of 6/30/2012. This project aims to help reduce youth risk of victimization through technology use (i.e., Internet, text messaging, webcams). It will survey a nationally representative sample of 1,500 youth to: 1) continue to track existing trends in the number and types of threats youth encounter using technology; 2) assess risks to youth of new behaviors and activities, including youth creating and distributing explicit images of themselves and/or peers; 3) assess benefits and utilization of safety programs and technologies, and 4) identify activities and behaviors most closely associated with risk. This study builds on a highly successful, decade-long research initiative at the Crimes against Children Research Center. Using a design refined in two previous Youth Internet Safety Surveys, a national probability sample of youth ages 10 through 17 will be interviewed by telephone about experiences with technology during the last 12 months. The design will allow direct comparison to findings from two previous surveys, providing valuable information on trends and new developments.

Multimedia Juvenile Victimization (MJV): Insights into Youth Behavior to Help Law Enforcement is a project designed by awardee, University of Hawaii. The award has a start date of 7/1/2009 and an end date of 6/30/2011. The Multimedia Juvenile Victimization (MJV): Insights into Youth Behavior to Help Law Enforcement project is a two-year study whose goal and purpose is to contribute to the understanding of Internet and technology-facilitated crimes against juveniles and assist law enforcement in their efforts to emulate youth behavior online, gather evidence, and prosecute violators, thereby addressing priority research area IV: Investigation of Internet Crimes and area

VI: Prevention Strategies. Major objectives are to determine prevalence and awareness of solicitous texting ("sexting") using cell phone text messaging, frequency of solicitation and distribution of explicit images using online social networks, and types of technologies used for cyberbullying. Participants are from three school districts—Hawaii, California, and Wyoming—with a fourth (Virginia) to be determined for the school year 2009-20 10. Data will be gathered via questionnaires distributed to a stratified random sample of each school district's student population, parents, and teachers.

Multi-Prong Approaches to Strengthening Internet Child Safety is a project designed by the awardee, Justice Resource Institute. The award has a start date of 10/1/2006 and an end date of 3/31/2010. The primary goal of this proposed research project is to reduce online sexual victimization of children and adolescents. A secondary goal of this project is to study the evolution and impact of adult and child pornography on Internet sexual offenders. This two-year project proposes to build on work supported by the Office of Juvenile Justice and Delinquency Prevention (OJJDP) in three important ways: (1) by conducting in-depth structured interviews of a large, diverse sample of Internet sexual offenders, (2) by examining the age spectrum of exposure to, use of, and technical familiarity with Internet pornography in high school students, college students and offenders, and (3) by reviewing the efficacy of existing child protection software with recommendations for the next "generation" of such filters. The purpose of this project is to advance the much-needed empirical research required to combat online sexual victimization of children and adolescents and improve Internet safety strategies.

Pathways to Commercial Sexual Victimization of Children-A Life Course Perspective is a project designed by the awardee, University of Massachusetts Lowell. The award has a start date of 9/1/2006 and an end date of 6/30/2009. The research will be an in-depth field-based study of CSEC taking a life course perspective in examining the lives of female and male victims, with a focus on prostituted teens. There will be a utilization of mixed-method and collaborative design to collect data that will uncover the dynamics of the sexual victimization and learn from the teens themselves more about the individual, family, peer, school, and community contexts of their victimization. The project has four specific aims: identify an appropriate group of adolescent girls and boys from whom we can directly elicit information to map out pathways into CSEC over this early but critical portion of the life course; refine an interview protocol that is currently in development based on FAIR und's pilot youth-led program.; interview 40 sexually victimized girls (prostituted girls), 20 boys sexually victimized via CSEC, and 40 run away youth (20 boys and 20 girls); facilitate utilization of findings beyond the Boston and Washington, D.C., by researchers, service providers and policy makers.

Victims No Longer: Research on Child Survivors of Trafficking for Sexual and Labor Exploitation in the United States, Final Report

NCJ 221891, Elzbieta Gozdziak Ph.D.; Micah N. Bump M. A., 2008, NIJ-Sponsored, (159 pages).

Commercial Sexual Exploitation of Children in New York City, Executive Summary

NCJ 225082, Ric Curtis; Karen Terry; Meredith Dank,; Kirk Dombrowski; Bilal Khan; Amy Muslim; Melissa Labriola; Michael Rempel, September 2008, NIJ-Sponsored, (14 pages).

Commercial Sexual Exploitation of Children in New York City, Volume Two: Formative Evaluation: The New York City Demonstration

NCJ 225084, Amy Muslim; Melissa Labriola; Michael Rempel, September 2008, NIJSponsored, (107 pages).

Evaluation of the Demonstration Project To Address Commercial Sexual Exploitation of Children in Atlanta-Fulton County

NCJ 226610, Mary Finn; Brenda Sims Blackwell; Leslie C. Jackson; James L. Wolk; M. Brooke Oakley, March 2009, NIJ-Sponsored, (301 pages).

Commercial Sexual Exploitation of Children: What Do We Know and What Do We Do About It?

NCJ 215733, Jay Albanese, December 2007, Report, NIJ, (20 pages).

Commercial Sexual Exploitation of Children in New York City, Volume One: The CSEC Population in New York City: Size, Characteristics, and Needs

NCJ 225083, Ric Curtis; Karen Terry; Meredith Dank; Kirk Dombrowski; Bilal Khan, September 2008, NIJ-Sponsored, (126 pages).

The National Institute of Justice (NIJ) is the research, development and evaluation agency of the U.S. Department of Justice and is dedicated to researching crime control and justice issues. NIJ provides objective, independent, evidence-based knowledge and tools to meet the challenges of crime and justice, particularly at the state and local levels. NIJ's principal authorities are derived from the Omnibus Crime Control and Safe Streets Act of 1968, as amended (see 42 USC § 372 13723) and Title II of the Homeland Security Act of 2002. NIJ is currently supporting the following research projects related to child exploitation.

Identifying Situational and Individual Risk Factors for Child Sexual Abuse in Institutional Settings: Implications for Public Safety and Primary Prevention awarded to John Jay College and supported jointly with the United States Conference on Catholic Bishops. A major barrier to prevention efforts has been the lack of information about the causes of child sexual abuse perpetration, specifically the interplay of individual, interpersonal, and situational factors that increase risk for the perpetration of sexual violence, especially when perpetrated by professionals in institutional contexts. The aims of this project are to (a) identify individual, relational, and situational risk and protective markers for sexual abuse perpetration in institutional settings, (b) build a taxonomic structure of clergy who sexually abuse children based upon these risk factors, and (c) develop a summary of *best practices* summarizing major research findings that can be distributed to faith based institutions and youth serving organizations.

Randomized Controlled Trial Study of a Parenting Intervention to Enhance Post-Release Adjustment and Reduce Recidivism for Reentering Fathers and their Children awarded to Child Trends and ICF International. This grant will examine the impact of adding an evidence-based parenting program to re-entry services for parents leaving prison. Among other factors the study will test whether the *Strengthening Family Program* (SFP) intervention improves family functioning, and reduces child maltreatment among this vulnerable population of re-entering fathers of children ages 6-21.

ARRA Process Evaluation of Current Internet Child Safety Activities by ICAC Task Forces awarded the University of New Hampshire. The investigators will conduct a multi-site evaluation of internet child safety materials used by Internet Crimes Against Children (ICAC) task forces in school- and community-based prevention and awareness programs.

Evaluation of O VC FY 09 Services to Domestic Minor Victims of Human Trafficking awarded to the Research Triangle Institute. The investigators will conduct a participatory process evaluation of three OVC demonstration programs that were chosen based on their promising strategies to deliver a comprehensive array of services to child victims (i.e., under age 18) of human trafficking who are U.S. citizens or legal permanent residents.

Adolescent Sexual Assault Victims' Experiences with SANE-SARTS and the Criminal Justice System awarded to Michigan State University. This study uses a multi method approach to learn about adolescent sexual assault survivors experiences with Sexual Assault Nurse Examiners (SANE). The study seeks to shed light on 1) Which cases make it through the system and why? 2) What role do SANE-SARTs play in encouraging victims to participate in prosecution? And 3) What are teen victim's concerns about seeking formal help initially?

Index

D

E

F

Q

R

S

T

U

V

W

Y